Folens

GCSE RELIGIOUS STUDIES
FOR EDEXCEL A — UNIT 8

RELIGION AND SOCIETY

BASED ON CHRISTIANITY AND ISLAM

endorsed by
edexcel

INA TAYLOR

Acknowledgements

p.8–9 © iStockphoto.com/Leif Norman; p.11 © Art Directors; p.13 © Art Directors; p.15 © Dawn/Fotolia; p.17 © David J. Green – Lifestyle/Alamy; p.18 © iStockphoto.com/Claudia Dewald; p.23 (top) © Sipa Press/Rex Features, (bottom left) © Liberty, www.liberty-human-rights.org.uk, (bottom right) © Liberty, www.liberty-human-rights.org.uk; p.24 © Art Directors; p25 (top) © ACAT UK, (bottom) © David Pearson /Alamy; p.26 (top) © Jennifer Westmoreland. Image from BigStockPhoto.com, (middle) © Claire Norman. Image from BigStockPhoto.com, (bottom) © iStockphoto.com/Dennis Owusu-Ansah; p.27 © Alistair Linford/Rex Features; p.28 © Digital Stock; p.32 © Victor de Schwanberg/Science Photo Library; p.33 © Jeremy Sutton Hibbert/Rex Features; p.34 © Makoto Iwafuji/Eurelios/Science Photo Library; p.35 (top) © CARE, (bottom) © Still Pictures/Sean Sprague; p.38–39 © iStockphoto.com/DNY59; p.40 Courtesy of Ina Taylor; p.41 (top) © Greenpeace, (bottom) © Operation Noah; p.42 © iStockphoto.com/Joy Fera; p.43 © Geoff Moore/Rex Features; p.44 © Greenpeace/Davison; p.45 © iStockphoto.com/Brasil2; p.47 © A Rocha International; p.48 © ARC; p.49 © LINE; p.52 © iStockphoto.com/digitalskillet; p.53 © Stuart Atkins/Rex Features; p.54 © Mauro Fermariello/Science Photo Library; p.55 © Skye Brackpool/Rex Features; p.56 © By Ian Miles-Flashpoint Pictures/Alamy; p.57 © Rex Features; p.60 © Rex Features; p.61 © Rex Features; p.62 © David Dominguez. Image from BigStockPhoto.com; p.63 © Jacek Bednarczyk/epa/Corbis; p.64 © Foch/Phanie/Rex Features; p.65 © Voisin/Phanie/Rex Features; p.68–69 © nstanev/Fotolia; p.70 © Peter Dejong/AP/PA Photos; p.71 © iStockphoto.com/SVLumagraphica; p.72 © Quaker Peace and Social Witness; p.73 (top) © EAPPI, (bottom) EAPPI/Thomas Meier; p.75 (top) © Sipa Press/Rex Features, (bottom) © Sipa Press/Rex Features; p.79 © Rex Features; p.80 © Sipa Press/Rex Features; p.81 © Danny Lawson/PA Archive/PA Photos; p.82 © Tony Kyriacou/Rex Features; p.83 © iStockphoto.com/Craig DeBourbon; p.84 © Paul Cotney/Alamy; p.85 (top) The Children's Society, (bottom) © Monkey Business/Fotolia; p.86 © Bubbles Photolibrary/Alamy; p.87 (top) © Beatbullying, (bottom) © Kidscape; p.90 © Ronald Grant Archive/BBC/FilmFour/Assassin Films; p.92 © Ronald Grant Archive/Universal Pictures; p.93 © David Pearson /Alamy; p.94 © ArkReligion.com; p.95 (top) © Kazuyoshi Nomachi/Corbis, (bottom) © ArkReligion.com; p.98–99 © iStockphoto.com/Marianna Bettini; p.100 © Matthew Polak/Sygma/Corbis; p.101 © Tony Baggett/Fotolia; p.103 © iStockphoto.com/William Mahar; p.104 Churches Advertising Network, www.churchads.org.uk; p.105 © Alamy/Jeff Morgan; p.106 © ArkReligion.com; p.107 © Islamic Relief; p.110 © Eamonn Clarke/allaction.co.uk /Eamonn and James Clarke/EMPICS Entertainment/PA Photos; p.111 © Amnesty International; p.112 © Digital Stock; p.113 © Dag Ohrlund/Rex Features; p.115 © Getty Images/AFP; p.118 © Jun Dangoy/Fotolia; p.119 © Rex Features; p.120 © Les Gibbon/Alamy; p.121 © Rex Features; p.122 © Pavel Raigorodski. Image from BigStockPhoto.com; p.123 The Salvation Army; p.125 © Adisa/Fotolia.

p.25 *Hope and Suffering: Sermons and Speeches*, Desmond Tutu (Fount, 1984); p.35 (top) CARE, www.care.org.uk, (bottom) From **What the Churches Say** 3rd Edn (CEM 2000) reproduced by permission of Christian Education; p.40–41 Greenpeace, www.greenpeace.org.uk; p.49 (top) *Islam and Ecology* (page ix). Ed. Fazlun Khalid with Joanne O'Brien. (New York, London: Cassell 1992) with the kind permission of the Alliance for Religions and Conservation, www.arcworld.org, © LINE; p.55 Catechism of the Catholic Church from www.vatican.va © Libreria Editrice Vaticana; p.61 Facts and figures adapted from 'Q&A: Organ donation laws', BBC NEWS, 17/11/2008; p.64 Quote from Mr Aiman Alzetani source 'QE surgeon takes Organ Donor Bus to Asian communities in Coventry', University Hospitals Birmingham NHS Foundation Trust, www.uhb.nhs.co.uk; p.65 'Difficult decisions for Hanif' based on 'When faith and medicine collide', BBC Berkshire, 30/05/2008; p.72 'Engaging with the Quaker testimonies: a toolkit' © Britain Yearly Meeting (Quakers) 2007; p.73 © Britain Yearly Meeting (Quakers) 2008; p.81 (top) Catholic Agency for Overseas Development (CAFOD), www.cafod.co.uk, (middle) Source: 'Cardinal Ratzinger, After the 9/11 Atttacks', Zenit 27/04/2005 © www.zenit.org; (bottom) © Britain Yearly Meeting (Quakers) 2008; p.110 Amnesty International; p.111 Amnesty International; p.113 Catechism of the Catholic Church from www.vatican.va © Libreria Editrice Vaticana; p.120 Alcohol Misuse: A briefing paper from the Church of England, www.cofe.anglican.org; p.122 The Salvation Army, www.salvationarmy.co.uk; p.125 Adapted from 'Muslim checkout staff get an alcohol opt-out clause', The Times, 30/09/2007 and 'Sainsbury Allows Muslim Cashiers to Refuse to Sell Alcoholic Beverages', Islam Today, 03/09/2007.

This material has been endorsed by Edexcel and offers high quality support for the delivery of Edexcel qualifications.

Edexcel endorsement does not mean that this material is essential to achieve any Edexcel qualification, nor does it mean that this is the only suitable material available to support any Edexcel qualification. No endorsed material will be used verbatim in setting any Edexcel examination and any resource lists produced by Edexcel shall include this and other appropriate texts. While this material has been through an Edexcel quality assurance process, all responsibility for the content remains with the publisher.

Copies of official specifications for all Edexcel qualifications may be found on the Edexcel website – www.edexcel.org.uk

Bible scriptures are taken from the Good News Bible published by The Bible Societies/Collins © American Bible Society.

© 2009 Ina Taylor.

United Kingdom: Folens Publishers, Waterslade House, Thame Road, Haddenham, Buckinghamshire, HP17 8NT.
Email: folens@folens.com Website: www.folens.com

Ireland: Folens Publishers, Greenhills Road, Tallaght, Dublin 24.
Email: info@folens.ie Website: www.folens.ie

Editor: Judi Hunter, Spellbound Books

Text design and layout: eMC Design Ltd., www.emcdesign.org.uk

Picture researcher: Sue Sharp

Cover design: Form, www.form.uk.com

Cover images: © Getty Images (above); © M Freeman / Photo Link / Stockbyte / Punchstock (below).

The websites recommended in this publication were correct at the time of going to press, however websites may have been removed or web addresses changed since that time. Folens has made every attempt to suggest websites that are reliable and appropriate for students' use. It is not unknown for unscrupulous individuals to put unsuitable material on websites that may be accessed by students. Teachers should check all websites before allowing students to access them. Folens is not responsible for the content of external websites.

For general spellings Folens adheres to Oxford Dictionary of English, Second Edition (Revised), 2005.

First published 2009 by Folens Limited.

Every effort has been made to contact copyright holders of material used in this publication. If any copyright holder has been overlooked, we will be pleased to make any necessary arrangements.

British Library Cataloguing in Publication Data. A catalogue record for this publication is available from the British Library.

ISBN 978-1-85008-436-5   Folens code FD4365.

Contents

Introduction

Some helpful tips about using this book

This textbook is designed to help you prepare for the Edexcel exam *Religion and Society Based on a Study of Christianity and at Least One Other Religion.* Because Islam is the other most popular religion schools choose to study, this book has chosen to look at Christianity and Islam in detail.

The exam requires you to study the relationship between religion and society especially in the UK and this book offers you plenty of up-to-date evidence to think about. Half of the course, and the exam, focus on learning and understanding the reasons people have for their beliefs and practices. The other half of the course challenges you to think about these issues for yourself and come to your own informed opinion about some very controversial subjects. In the exam, you will be asked to express your opinion and give the reasons for your viewpoint.

How does the book work?

The book has been designed to follow the exam specification very closely. It is divided into four chapters.

Chapter 1 Rights and responsibilities

This chapter must only be based on a study of Christianity. You will be studying the different sources of authority Christians use when making a moral decision. You will study the reasons why Christians believe these sources offer guidance and how Christians use them. You will also examine the issue of human rights in the UK and democratic and electoral processes in the UK. This chapter studies the reasons why Christians believe human rights are important and analyses some biblical teachings about moral duties and responsibilities. You will go on to examine the nature of genetic engineering and cloning, and then consider different Christian responses to these very controversial subjects.

Chapter 2 Environmental and medical issues

This chapter of study also contains some very controversial issues that will give you plenty to argue about! It begins with discussions about the way humans are exploiting the planet. This includes a study of global warming, pollution and the way natural resources are becoming scarcer as a result of human activity. You will go on to examine the issue of fertility treatment and different people's reactions to it, including Christians and Muslims. This is followed by the equally controversial subject of transplant surgery, where you will investigate what it means and why some people believe it is important. Then you will examine different religious and non-religious attitudes towards transplant surgery.

Chapter 3 Peace and conflict

In this chapter you will be studying why conflicts arise and how they might be resolved. This involves a study of the work of the United Nations and some international conflicts. You will examine different attitudes to war within Christianity and Islam and the reasons these religions give for their views. Looking at conflict on a smaller scale, you will consider what these two religions think about bullying and how religious conflicts can arise within families. The chapter ends with a study of Christian and Muslim teachings about the importance of forgiveness and reconciliation.

Chapter 4 Crime and punishment

Here you will be looking at the need for laws and justice in a society and how people deal with those who break the rules. You will examine the reasons why Christians and Muslims think justice is important. This is followed by the controversial subject of capital punishment (the death penalty). You will weigh up the reasons for and against capital punishment put forward by Christians, Muslims and people of no religion. The chapter ends with an examination of the problems caused by drugs and alcohol and a study of the law on their misuse. You will consider the different attitudes Christians and Muslims have towards drugs and alcohol.

Topic pages

The pages have been designed with lots of features to make learning each topic lively and memorable.

Keywords

Each chapter contains 12 keywords and these appear on the opening pages of each chapter. They appear again as you work through the chapter to help you become familiar with them. They are also collected in the back of the book, in a Keyword glossary.

Quotations

These are taken from holy books. Using them could impress your examiner.

Activities

The activities reinforce your learning. You can work on them individually or tackle them as a class.

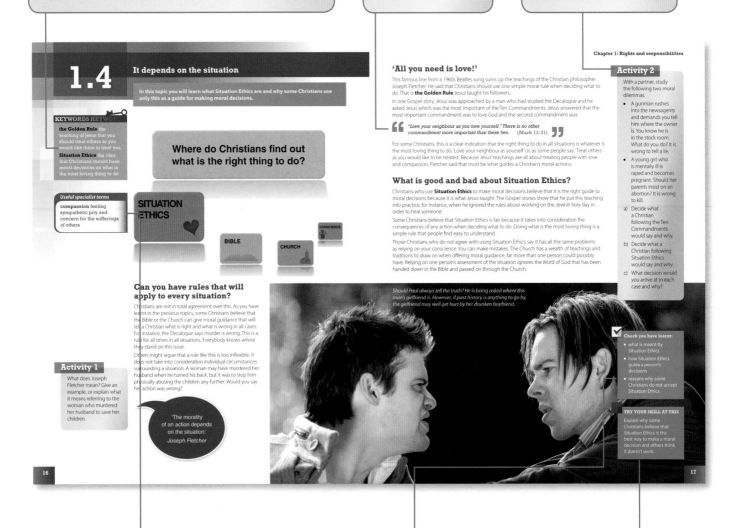

Useful specialist terms

You will not be asked to give the meaning of these words, but you can boost your marks by using them correctly in your exam answers.

Check you have learnt

This asks you to summarize what you have learnt about each topic, so you can check you've grasped the key points.

Try your skill at this

These questions will give you an opportunity to practise your newly-learnt skills with exam-style questions, building up your knowledge and confidence.

Giving you plenty of coaching

In order to help you get the best possible grades that you can, there is plenty of help with improving your exam skills. Within every chapter of study there are three Skills coaching spreads. These are designed to help you become familiar with the four different types of questions you will see on the exam paper.

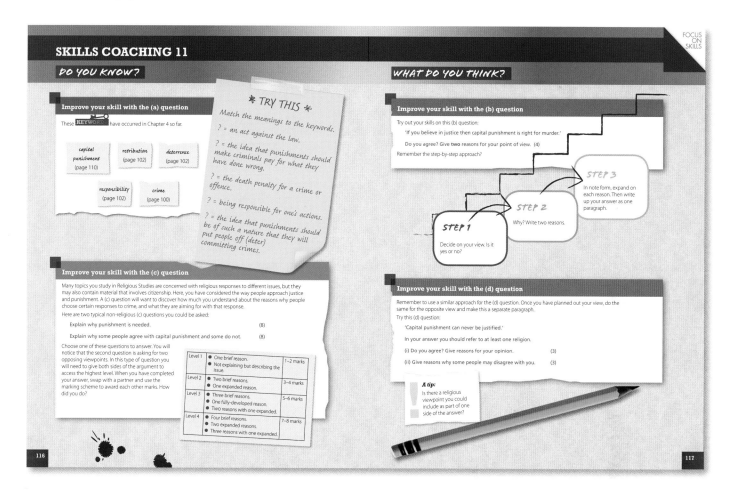

The left-hand page is called 'Do you know?' because it concentrates on the two questions that test your knowledge and understanding of what you have learnt. This skill carries half the marks. The right-hand page is called 'What do you think?' because it helps you to give your views and reasons. These two questions carry the other half of the marks on the paper.

There will be analysis of the questions so you get used to understanding exactly what the examiner is looking for. You will also look closely at the way the examiner marks each type of question with examples of the marking grids that are used. For each type of question, you will get step-by-step help with constructing an answer plus a few chances to 'Be the examiner' yourself. On these occasions you will be reading someone else's answer, comparing it with the marking criteria, and then awarding a grade and giving the student a few tips on improving their marks!

Each End of Chapter Check reminds you of what you should have learnt in that chapter and contains a practice exam page for you to try out.

This is a very exciting course of study with plenty of material to grab your attention and get you arguing. Enjoy!

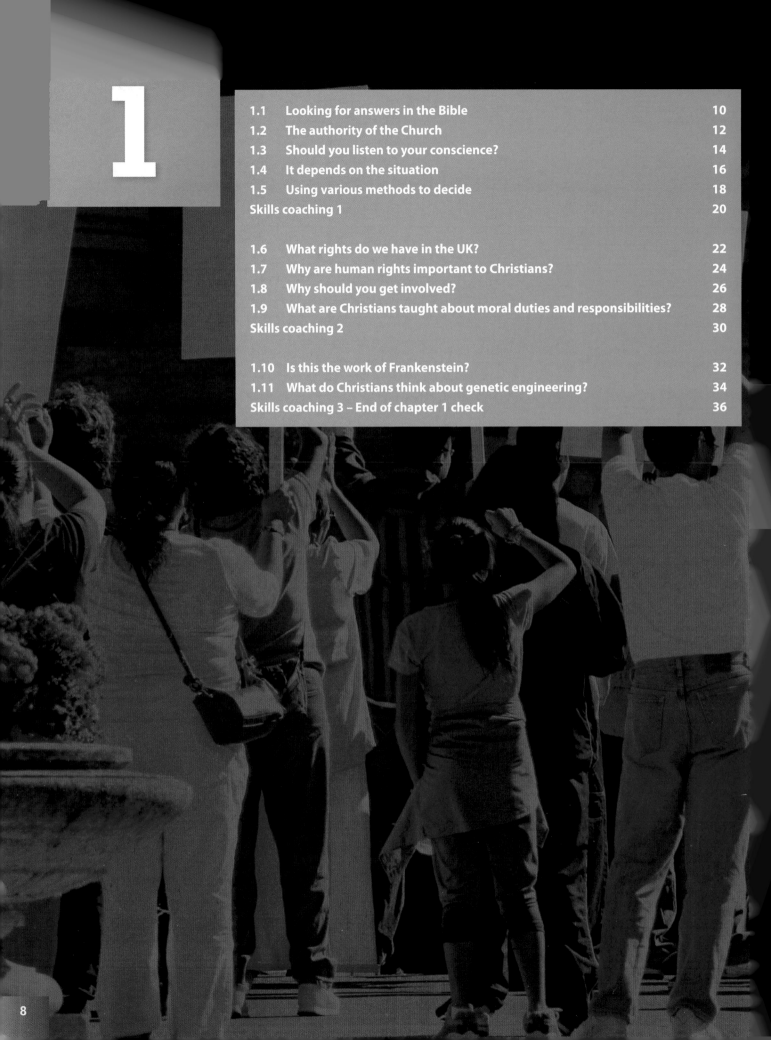

1

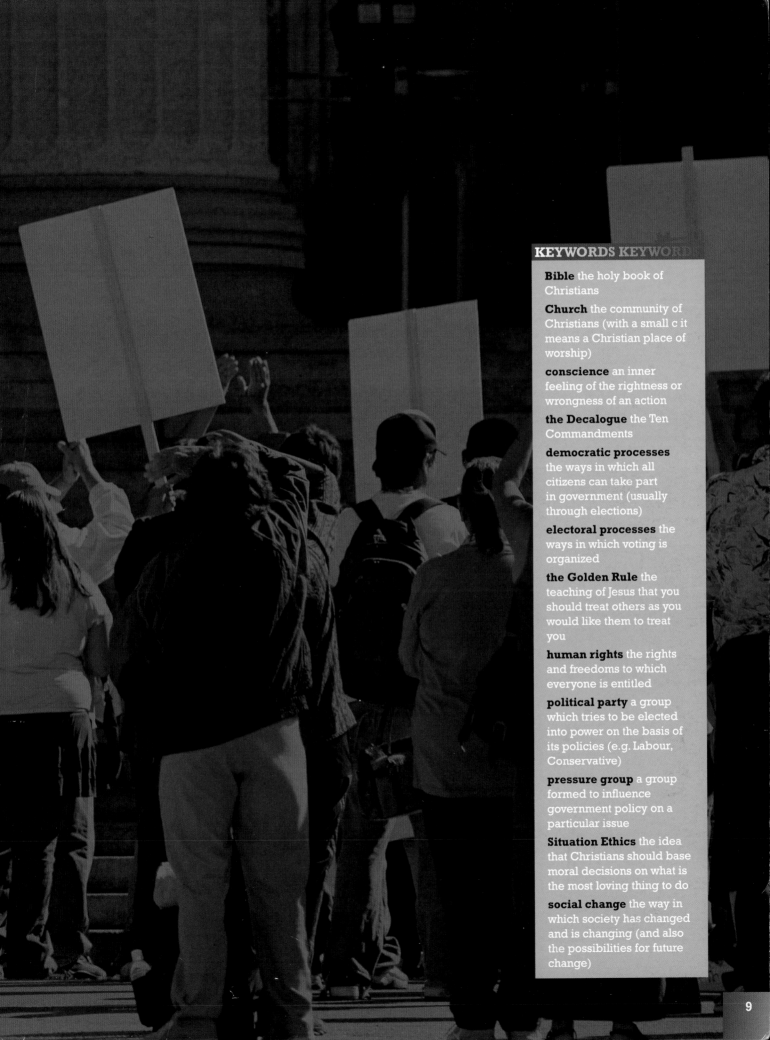

KEYWORDS KEYWORD

Bible the holy book of Christians

Church the community of Christians (with a small c it means a Christian place of worship)

conscience an inner feeling of the rightness or wrongness of an action

the Decalogue the Ten Commandments

democratic processes the ways in which all citizens can take part in government (usually through elections)

electoral processes the ways in which voting is organized

the Golden Rule the teaching of Jesus that you should treat others as you would like them to treat you

human rights the rights and freedoms to which everyone is entitled

political party a group which tries to be elected into power on the basis of its policies (e.g. Labour, Conservative)

pressure group a group formed to influence government policy on a particular issue

Situation Ethics the idea that Christians should base moral decisions on what is the most loving thing to do

social change the way in which society has changed and is changing (and also the possibilities for future change)

Looking for answers in the Bible

In this topic you will examine the way some Christians use only the Bible as a basis for making moral decisions.

How do you know what is right and what is wrong?

It is easy for people to say, 'You should do the right thing,' but how does anybody know what's right and what's wrong? What is needed is a source of authority that is easily accessible and totally reliable.

Christians look to God as the ultimate source of authority to decide what is right and what is wrong. This might seem straightforward enough, except, as you will see over the next few topics, Christians look in different places to consult God's authority. This diagram shows some of the places.

Where do Christians find out what is the right thing to do?

BIBLE

CHURCH

CONSCIENCE

SITUATION ETHICS

Look in a book

For hundreds of years, books have been accepted as the best source of authority. People trust what they see in print, believing it has stood the test of time. Today, the computer has largely taken its place as a method of checking facts. Where would you automatically look if you had to find out the date of the first printed copy of the Bible? Whilst it is likely you would use the Internet, you'd probably be looking at the written word on screen – an electronic book in effect.

For some Christians, the **Bible** is the best source of authority.

What makes the Bible special?

Christians believe that the Bible is no ordinary book because it was inspired by God. This means that what is written there has God's authority. The Bible, which has been in existence for hundreds of years, contains rules and teachings telling people how to lead their lives. These are the parts some Christians turn to when they need answers to difficult moral questons.

- **The rules** – Christians are most likely to consult the Ten Commandments, also known as **the Decalogue**. Some Christians regard these as God-given rules. They are found in the Old Testament part of the Bible. Also found there are many other rules about the way people should behave.

- **The teachings** – for Christians, the most important teachings are those given by Jesus, the Son of God, and these are found in the New Testament. Jesus' Sermon on the Mount tells followers about the sort of lives God wants people to lead. Jesus told many parables, or stories, to help people understand his teachings better. Christians also read the teachings of St Paul, who lived after Jesus and wrote a large number of letters to assist newly-formed Christian groups to make the right moral decisions.

Different attitudes towards the authority of the Bible

- For some Christians, the Bible contains the words of God, quite literally. This means that the Bible must be consulted and followed as closely as possible.

- Other Christians consult the Bible but interpret it for today's society. They say that, although God inspired the Bible, humans wrote the words down hundreds of years ago to help the society they lived in. Times have changed and God's message needs adapting for the twenty-first century. For instance, attitudes towards women or concern about animals, have changed greatly over the past 2000 years.

- Other Christians regard the Bible mainly as the source of authority for Church leaders to study and then pass on God's message to worshippers. (You will study this in more detail on pages 12–13.)

Activity 1

a) Look up the Ten Commandments in Exodus 20:1–17. Briefly list the ten rules.

b) What moral guidance is there for Shelley who is thinking of leaving her husband for a man she met at the gym?

Activity 2

Make a poster showing the importance of the Bible as a source of authority for Christians.

The Decalogue, or Ten Commandments, can be seen on the walls of many churches. This shows how important Christians have found it for making moral decisions.

✓ **Check you have learnt:**

- why the Bible is an important source of authority
- what parts of the Bible are used in making moral decisions
- differences in Christian attitudes to the authority of the Bible.

TRY YOUR SKILL AT THIS

Explain why some Christians would say that the Bible is all they need to make moral decisions.

In this topic you will learn about the authority of the Church for Christians, and why some Christians use only the Church's teachings as a basis for making moral decisions.

Church the community of Christians (with a small c it means a Christian place of worship)

Useful specialist terms

clergy trained priests in the Christian Church

laity the ordinary members of a Christian community

magisterium the teaching authority of the Roman Catholic Church, which provides guidance on moral issues

infallible guidance unchangeable rules given to members of the Roman Catholic Church by the Pope

Where do Christians find out what is the right thing to do?

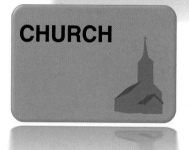

CHURCH

CONSCIENCE

SITUATION ETHICS

BIBLE

What is meant by the Church?

People often think of a building when they talk of the church and that is correct. The Christian place of worship is a church, written with a small c. What is far more important than any building of stone or brick is the people who worship in the place. These are also called the **Church** with a capital c.

The Christian Church is made up of the clergy, who are trained priests, and the laity, who are the ordinary worshippers.

How does the priest know what is right?

A priest will have spent several years training and, during this time, will have studied the Bible and learnt how the Church has interpreted certain passages. This enables priests to help members of their community if they ask for advice about a moral problem.

Activity 1

Explain why a Christian couple who want to know whether it is right to have fertility treatment might ask a priest.

How does the Church decide what is right?

Many issues have been discussed and prayed over for centuries, which has led Church leaders to an understanding about how God intends his followers to behave. These teachings have become part of the Christian tradition priests learn about.

More recent moral issues, like the rights and wrongs of fertility treatment, are prayed about by leaders in the Church. Christians believe that God guides present-day Church leaders to arrive at the correct teachings about moral issues, which are then passed on to the Christian community.

Protestant Churches, like the Church of England and the Methodists, elect members to meet as an assembly to discuss moral issues. They try to agree on the teachings priests can pass on to their congregation. In 2008, two difficult moral issues that occupied the assembly of the Church of England were whether it was acceptable to have homosexual clergy and whether women could become bishops.

In the Roman Catholic Church, the magisterium gives official teachings on moral issues to Catholics. These teachings are issued by the Pope (the head of the Catholic Church) and the Council of Bishops. They believe their decisions are guided by the Holy Spirit. The guidance on a moral issue may be published in the Catholic Catechism or issued as an official letter from the Pope. In a few exceptional cases, the Pope may give infallible guidance to Catholics on certain issues. An infallible rule can never ever be altered because Catholics believe that the Pope's ruling has come directly from God.

Where does the Church get its authority from?

Many Christians believe that God continues to guide people in the world through the Church. Some Christians regard the Church as the Body of Christ alive in the world today. This means that the Church has the same authority as that of Jesus.

Other Christians believe that God can make his will known to ordinary members of the congregation, which gives the community of believers great authority.

As Christian leaders, the clergy have training and experience that enable them to give authoritative guidance on moral issues to the laity. A few Christians believe that God can speak directly through priests, whilst others believe a priest's special training and relationship with God enable him to interpret scriptures reliably.

Christians who look to the Church for guidance on moral issues, rather than relying on their own interpretation of the Bible, argue that it is not only more reliable but holds the Christian community together.

Activity 2

Draw a diagram showing the different ways the Church passes moral guidance from God to the laity.

Here you can see the Church coming out of the church! The church (with a small c) is the building these people are coming from and the community of Christians emerging from the building is called the Church (with a capital c).

☑ **Check you have learnt:**

- what is meant by Church
- where the Church gets its authority from
- why some Christians believe that the Church is the most reliable source of moral guidance.

TRY YOUR SKILL AT THIS

Explain why some Christians believe that the Church's teachings are the best source of moral guidance.

In this topic you will learn about the role of the conscience, and why some Christians believe that the conscience is the most important guide in making ethical decisions.

Where do Christians find out what is the right thing to do?

CONSCIENCE

SITUATION ETHICS

BIBLE

CHURCH

What is your conscience?

Everyone, whether religious or not, knows instinctively when they have done something wrong and they usually feel guilty. We usually say it is our **conscience** telling us. The conscience is an inner feeling that seems to know instinctively what is right and what is wrong about an action, whether we like what we are being told or not! Conscience doesn't just tell us something is wrong, it also prompts us that a certain action, perhaps going over to talk to a new arrival in the class, is the right thing to do. Our conscience doesn't *make* us do anything, it simply informs. That is the idea behind the picture of the policeman who is just observing what is going on and knows whether it is right or wrong. As humans, we are free to choose how we act.

Where does conscience come from?

Christians believe that our conscience is an inner part given to us by God as guidance. Some interpret the conscience as the voice of the Holy Spirit, leading them towards doing the right thing. For these Christians, the conscience is the most important guide anyone can have when it comes to making moral decisions.

Activity 1

Invent **three** moral issues where you think a person's conscience could lead them to do the right thing.

Some Christians think that our conscience is like a policeman quietly watching and judging our thoughts and actions.

How reliable a guide is conscience?

Some Christians would say our conscience is the most reliable guide we have when it comes to making moral decisions because it is led by God. They point out that there are many actions like theft, murder or rape which are universally wrong. Everyone knows this, whatever culture, religion or century they live in.

Non-religious people would also say there is universal agreement that certain actions are good and others bad, though they say it is reason and experience that have taught our conscience the rules, not God.

On the other hand …

There have been a few notable examples of people claiming to be following their conscience, yet acting in the most horrific manner. Peter Sutcliffe, the Yorkshire Ripper, claimed to have been led by the voice of God to kill prostitutes. Instances like this are rare and it is often the case that the person has mental health problems. What it highlights, though, is the fact that conscience is a personal matter. What happens if someone's conscience directs them to do things most people don't agree with?

Activity 2

Work with a partner to see if you can think of a moral dilemma where a person's conscience might be torn between **two** possible solutions. Share your thoughts with the group to see what they think. Would you say this makes a person's conscience a useless guide or not?

Activity 3

Read the following extract. Explain what the Roman Catholic Church is telling its followers about using conscience as a guide to making moral decisions.

> *In all his activity a man is bound to follow conscience faithfully, in order that he may come to God for whom he was created. It follows that he is not to be forced to act in a manner contrary to his conscience.*
>
> **(Declaration on Religious Freedom, Vatican II)**

Check you have learnt:

- what is meant by conscience
- how the conscience can guide moral decisions
- the strengths and weaknesses of relying on your conscience alone for guidance.

Activity 4

Draw a line down your page. Head one column 'Advantages' and the other 'Problems'. With a partner, discuss and write down the advantages and problems that might arise if people only used their conscience as the basis for all moral decisions.

TRY YOUR SKILL AT THIS

Do you think that laws could be abolished if everybody acted according to their conscience?

Give **two** reasons for your point of view.

In this topic you will learn what Situation Ethics are and why some Christians use only this as a guide for making moral decisions.

the Golden Rule the teaching of Jesus that you should treat others as you would like them to treat you

Situation Ethics the idea that Christians should base moral decisions on what is the most loving thing to do

Useful specialist terms

compassion feeling sympathetic pity and concern for the sufferings of others

Where do Christians find out what is the right thing to do?

SITUATION ETHICS

 **BIBLE**

 **CHURCH**

 CONSCIENCE

Can you have rules that will apply to every situation?

Christians are not in total agreement over this. As you have learnt in the previous topics, some Christians believe that the Bible or the Church can give moral guidance that will tell a Christian what is right and what is wrong in all cases. For instance, the Decalogue says murder is wrong. This is a rule for all times in all situations. Everybody knows where they stand on this issue.

Others might argue that a rule like this is too inflexible. It does not take into consideration individual circumstances surrounding a situation. A woman may have murdered her husband when he turned his back, but it was to stop him physically abusing the children any further. Would you say her action was wrong?

Activity 1

What does Joseph Fletcher mean? Give an example, or explain what it means referring to the woman who murdered her husband to save her children.

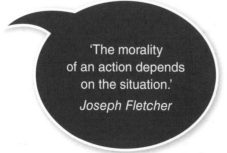

'The morality of an action depends on the situation.'
Joseph Fletcher

'All you need is love!'

This famous line from a 1960s Beatles song sums up the teachings of the Christian philosopher Joseph Fletcher. He said that Christians should use one simple moral rule when deciding what to do. That is **the Golden Rule** Jesus taught his followers.

In one Gospel story, Jesus was approached by a man who had studied the Decalogue and he asked Jesus which was the most important of the Ten Commandments. Jesus answered that the most important commandment was to love God and the second commandment was:

> *"Love your neighbour as you love yourself." There is no other commandment more important than these two.* **(Mark 12:31)**

For some Christians, this is a clear indication that the right thing to do in all situations is whatever is the most loving thing to do. 'Love your neighbour as yourself' or, as some people say, 'Treat others as you would like to be treated'. Because Jesus' teachings are all about treating people with love and compassion, Fletcher said that must be what guides a Christian's moral actions.

What is good and bad about Situation Ethics?

Christians who use **Situation Ethics** to make moral decisions believe that it is the right guide to moral decisions because it is what Jesus taught. The Gospel stories show that he put this teaching into practice, for instance, when he ignored the rules about working on the Jewish holy day in order to heal someone.

Some Christians believe that Situation Ethics is fair because it takes into consideration the consequences of any action when deciding what to do. Doing what is the most loving thing is a simple rule that people find easy to understand.

Those Christians who do not agree with using Situation Ethics say it has all the same problems as relying on your conscience. You can make mistakes. The Church has a wealth of teachings and traditions to draw on when offering moral guidance, far more than one person could possibly have. Relying on one person's assessment of the situation ignores the Word of God that has been handed down in the Bible and passed on through the Church.

Activity 2

With a partner, study the following two moral dilemmas.

- A gunman rushes into the newsagents and demands you tell him where the owner is. You know he is in the stock room. What do you do? It is wrong to tell a lie.
- A young girl who is mentally ill is raped and becomes pregnant. Should her parents insist on an abortion? It is wrong to kill.

a) Decide what a Christian following the Ten Commandments would say and why.

b) Decide what a Christian following Situation Ethics would say and why.

c) What decision would you arrive at in each case and why?

Should Paul always tell the truth? He is being asked where this man's girlfriend is. However, if past history is anything to go by, the girlfriend may well get hurt by her drunken boyfriend.

✓ **Check you have learnt:**

- what is meant by Situation Ethics
- how Situation Ethics guide a person's decisions
- reasons why some Christians do not accept Situation Ethics.

TRY YOUR SKILL AT THIS

Explain why some Christians believe that Situation Ethics is the best way to make a moral decision and others think it doesn't work.

In this topic you will consider why some Christians use a variety of authorities in making moral decisions.

Where do Christians find out what is the right thing to do?

Activity 1

a) Why do some Christians like the flexibility of using various sources of authority?

b) Why do some Christians prefer one source of authority for moral decisions?

BIBLE

Advantages:
- It is clearly set down in writing.
- It was inspired by God.
- Bibles are easily available for Christians to read and get answers for themselves.

Disadvantages:
- The Bible is a large book and not easy to understand.
- A Christian may not find an example of the same moral problem.
- The Bible was written down hundreds of years ago.

What sort of sources of authority could a Christian use for guidance about whether or not it is right to switch off the life support of this patient who is brain-dead?

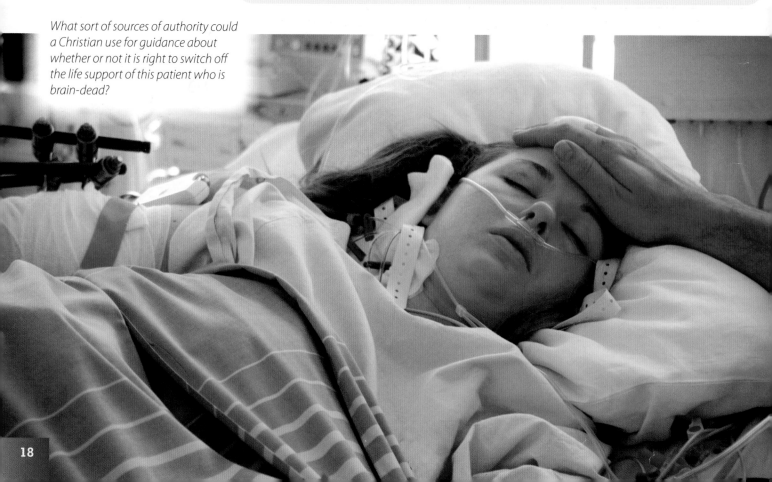

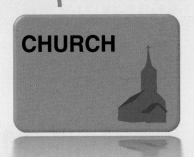

CHURCH

Advantages:

- The Church has many centuries of experience and tradition to draw on, which keeps Christians united.
- Some Christians prefer to seek help from professional clergy.
- Clear guidance can be given and Christians don't have to worry about getting it wrong.

Disadvantages:

- Some Christians may not have easy access to clergy.
- Some Christians may disagree with the Church's ruling.
- There is no flexibility.

CONSCIENCE

Advantages:

- Everybody has a conscience.
- There is general agreement about what is right and wrong.
- It is easy to consult.

Disadvantages:

- Some people's conscience may lead them astray.
- Some issues are too complicated for people to be sure about what their conscience is saying.
- It is helpful to have outside help.

SITUATION ETHICS

Advantages:

- The rule is simple to apply.
- It takes into account all aspects of a situation.
- It follows Jesus' teachings.

Disadvantages:

- People may disagree about what is the most loving thing to do.
- Some moral dilemmas are too complicated to be solved this way.
- It can take too long to weigh everything up when a quick decision is needed.

The diagram shows that all these major sources of authority have their advantages and disadvantages. For some Christians, this is not a problem. The authority they decide on provides clear, reliable guidance that they believe is right. This can be a great help because it removes the worry and responsibility about what they should do.

Other Christians believe that there is no 'one size fits all' solution. Because moral dilemmas are often complicated, they may require different approaches. So it is quite common for Christians to use a variety of different authorities depending on the situation they are faced with. They do not regard that as a weakness. All the authorities shown in the diagram rely on God for their ultimate authority. The Christian is simply seeking God's guidance in the most accessible form at that moment.

Activity 2

With a partner, read the different cases below and decide which is the best source of moral guidance for a Christian in each case, and why.

a) A twenty-pound note has been left on the floor in the classroom. How will a Christian know what to do about it?

b) Your mum comes in wearing an absolutely hideous skirt. She asks you if it suits her. If you were a Christian, how would you react? What source of authority do you think offers the best guidance?

c) You hear a juicy piece of gossip about one of the girls in your class. You have no idea if it is true but your mates would love to hear it. If you were a Christian, how would you decide what is the right thing to do?

d) One Christian wants to get divorced because his wife is having an affair. His wife doesn't want to get divorced because she promised to remain married until death parted them. How will they know what is the right thing to do?

✓ Check you have learnt:

- four different authorities Christians might use when making a moral decision
- the advantages of each authority
- the disadvantages of each authority.

TRY YOUR SKILL AT THIS

'Having a variety of different ways of making moral decisions is just confusing for Christians.'

(i) Do you agree? Give reasons for your opinion.

(ii) Give reasons why some people may disagree with you.

DO YOU KNOW?

One important area the exam will be testing is your knowledge and understanding of the material you have studied. The (a) and (c) questions do this.

The (a) question – KEY WORDS

The simplest form of knowledge appears in the (a) part of every question and asks you to give the meaning of a keyword. That's easy! There are only 12 keywords in each chapter. Take the time to learn them so you can collect your **2 marks** every time.

Check your knowledge of these keywords that you have already learnt:

Bible
(page 10)

the Decalogue
(page10)

Church
(page 12)

Situation Ethics
(page 16)

conscience
(page 14)

the Golden Rule
(page 16)

✳ **MIX AND MATCH** ✳
Write each of the six keywords and their meanings on a separate slip of paper. Cut out each keyword and meaning separately. Shuffle them and try matching each keyword to its correct meaning. Turn it into a game with your partner and see who can score the most marks.

The (c) question

This question is testing more than just your knowledge; it is testing whether you actually *understand* what you have learnt.

This question will usually have the word *Explain* … in it because the examiner is asking you to give reasons. It may even say *Explain with examples*. Here is a typical example of a (c) question:

> Explain why some Christians use a variety of authorities when making a moral decision. (8)

Because **8 marks** are on offer for this question, it is clear the examiner is expecting you to give more than one reason. Aim to write three or four reasons and express them in your best written English – some of the marks are also being awarded for your **Q**uality of **W**ritten **C**ommunication (known as **QWC**).

Try your skill with this (c) question or the one above.

> Explain why some Christians think all moral decisions should be based on the most loving thing to do. (8)

Try it in easy steps:

STEP 1
Copy the question down and underline the most important words.

STEP 2
Jot down as many reasons as you can think of. If your memory is shaky, look back to pages 16–19 to see what reasons were given.

STEP 3
Take each point and develop it into a full sentence, expanding it with more detail if you can.

WHAT DO YOU THINK?

In the (b) and the (d) questions you are asked for your opinion. The important thing to remember here is that you have to back up your opinion with a reason. Nobody's opinion counts for much if they can't tell you why. Remember: **'I think this … because …'.**

The (b) question

Here you will read something controversial like:

Do you think it is always best to do exactly what the Church says?

Then the examiner will ask for your opinion and **two reasons** why you think this. Obviously, if you just wrote a one-word answer like 'No' or 'Yes', you wouldn't get any marks. You are bound to have reasons for your opinion, so write them down. It's as simple as that!

Try your skill at this (b) question or the one above:

Do you think the Bible is the best source of authority for Christians?

Give **two** reasons for your point of view. (4)

The (d) question

The (d) question is really a development of the (b) question because it starts in the same way. You will be given a quotation such as 'If everybody followed their conscience, we wouldn't need laws.' Then you will be asked:

(i) Do you agree? Give reasons for your opinion. (3)

The (d) question then goes on to test whether you can understand someone else's point of view by asking:

(ii) Explain why some people may disagree with you. (3)

Because this is a Religious Studies paper, you must refer to a religious point of view in at least **one** side of your argument.

Try your skill with this (d) question:

'If everybody followed their conscience, we wouldn't need laws.'

In your answer you should refer to Christianity.

(i) Do you agree? Give reasons for your opinion. (3)

(ii) Explain why some people may disagree with you. (3)

In this topic you will look at human rights in the UK.

What are human rights?

We are so used to people claiming 'It's my right' to do something or 'I've got my rights'. But what do they really mean? And is it true? What **human rights** do people have? By human rights, we mean a freedom and entitlement to something in life.

Although the UK has a long history of concern for the abuse of human rights, the Human Rights Act has only had a place in British law since 1998.

KEYWORDS KEYWORDS

human rights the rights and freedoms to which everyone is entitled

Activity 1

With a partner, list **ten** things you both agree a person is entitled to simply because they are human.

The Universal Declaration of Human Rights

After the human rights abuses of World War II, the United Nations (UN) drew up this declaration in 1948. The full text can be read on the UN's website, but here are the main points:

1 Right to equality.
2 Freedom from discrimination.
3 Right to life, liberty and personal security.
4 Freedom from slavery.
5 Freedom from torture or degrading treatment.
6 Right to be recognized as a person by the law.
7 Right to equality before the law.
8 Right to a fair hearing if your rights are broken.
9 Freedom from arrest with no reason and exile.
10 Right to a fair public hearing if accused of something illegal.
11 Right to be considered innocent until proven guilty.
12 Freedom from interference with privacy, family, home and correspondence.
13 Right to free movement in and out of the country.
14 Right to asylum in other countries if being persecuted at home.
15 Right to a nationality and the freedom to change it.
16 Right to marriage and family.
17 Right to own property.
18 Freedom of belief and religion.
19 Freedom of opinion and information.
20 Right to meet peacefully with others and join groups.
21 Right to participate in government by voting and standing for election.
22 Right to social security.
23 Right to work safely for equal pay and to join a trade union.
24 Right to rest and leisure.
25 Right to an adequate living standard.
26 Right to an education.
27 Right to participate in cultural activity, e.g. the arts.
28 Right to have society run in a way which protects your rights.
29 Everyone has duties but these should only help achieve everyone's rights in society, they cannot harm rights.
30 Everyone should be free from interference in their rights.

This Declaration is not the law in its own right, but it affected the terms of the 1950 European Convention on Human Rights which does have legal status, as does the European Court of Human Justice set up nine years later. Everyone resident in Europe can appeal to this court for justice against the actions of their own government. In 1998, the UK Human Rights Act incorporated the European Convention on Human Rights into British law.

Courts in the UK

In Britain, every UK citizen is entitled to the human rights listed here because they are enshrined in law. If a person feels that their human rights have been abused, they can take their case to court. Here a judge and jury will listen to the evidence and decide on the legality of the situation. The jury consists of 12 ordinary citizens of the country, which shows everybody has a responsibility for human rights.

If the person bringing the case does not agree with the verdict of the UK court, they have the right to take their case to the European court.

Diane Pretty asked the UK court to allow her husband to help her die because she was suffering from a terminal illness. She believed that it was her human right to be able to choose how she died. When she lost this case, she took it to the European Court of Human Justice, but they also refused to grant her husband freedom from prosecution for murder.

Are everybody's human rights protected in the UK?

Yes, if they are a British or European citizen. There continues to be a lot of debate over whether or not migrants are entitled to the same rights as UK citizens. In September 2008, the British government was severely criticized by the UN for locking up children of migrants in detention centres. The government was shamed into changing its policy and migrant children were granted the same human rights as children born in the UK.

Similar battles continue to be fought to gain basic human rights for migrant girls illegally brought into the UK and forced into the sex trade.

LIBERTY
PROTECTING CIVIL LIBERTIES
PROMOTING HUMAN RIGHTS

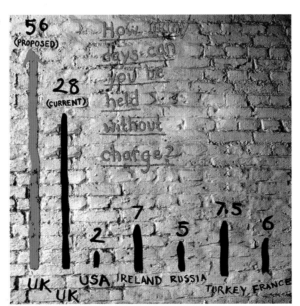

In 2007 the human rights group Liberty produced research comparing pre-charge detention limits (the period of time that an individual can be held and questioned by police before being charged with an offence) around the world.

✓ **Check you have learnt:**
- what is meant by human rights
- what the UN Human Rights Act is
- what the UK does to promote human rights.

TRY YOUR SKILL AT THIS

The (b) question:

'Everybody is entitled to human rights in the UK.'

Do you agree? Give **two** reasons for your point of view. (4)

In this topic you will examine the reasons why human rights are important to Christians.

Bible teachings

There are many biblical passages that teach Christians the importance of human rights. In the very first book of the Bible, Genesis, it says: 'Adam named his wife Eve, because she was the mother of all human beings' (Genesis 3:20), which shows that we are all related. Modern science agrees. If everybody is related, then it means they are all entitled to the same rights – human rights.

Jesus was concerned

Jesus' teachings and behaviour also teach Christians the importance of human rights. The famous story of The Good Samaritan (Luke 10:25–37) shows that the way a person acts towards fellow humans is what matters most, not the type of person they are. The hero of the story was a Samaritan, who came from an area where Jews thought second-class citizens lived.

The Gospels also tell of times when Jesus went out of his way to ensure people who had been rejected by everyone else received a fair treatment. There are accounts of him healing a leper whom nobody would go near, of dealing kindly with a prostitute and a tax collector, as well as responding to a request for help from a Roman soldier. All of these people would have been disliked by Jewish society and ignored if possible.

Christians might put their concern about human rights into practice by buying goods that they know have been fairly traded. There is concern that many products we buy cheaply in the UK have actually been produced by workers on low wages in appalling conditions. This is an abuse of their human rights, which the Bible teaches Christians is unacceptable.

Activity 1

What does the following biblical passage teach a Christian about human rights?

 From one human being he created all races on earth and made them live throughout the whole earth. **(Acts 17:26)**

Christian responses

The Catholic Church believes human rights matter:

 Each individual is truly a person, with a nature that is endowed with intelligence and free will, and rights and duties ... these rights and duties are universal and inviolable.

(Pope John XXIII)

The Christian charity, Action by Christians Against Torture (ACAT), was formed in 1984 to fight a particular form of human rights abuse.

Here is a biblical quote that features on their website:

> *Remember those who are in prison, as though you were in prison with them; those who are being tortured, as though you yourselves were being tortured.* **(Hebrews 13:3)**

Activity 2

Read the ACAT prayer which you can find on their website. According to this prayer why should Christians fight for the human rights of prisoners?

Activity 3

a) Look at ACAT's website. Report on **two** things they are doing about this specific form of human rights abuse.

b) What motivates them as Christians to do this work?

Archbishop Desmond Tutu has been an outspoken critic of human rights abuse. He campaigned against the way the white South African government treated black South Africans as second-class citizens.

Desmond Tutu said:

"Christian worship can never let us be indifferent to the needs of others, to the cries of the hungry, of the naked and the homeless, of the sick and the prisoner, of the oppressed and the disadvantaged. If it were not for faith, I am certain lots of us would have been hate-filled and bitter … But to speak of God, you must speak of your neighbour … He does not tolerate a relationship with himself that excludes your neighbour."

✓ Check you have learnt:

- one biblical reason why Christians are concerned about human rights
- what inspiration Jesus gives Christians
- an example of a modern-day Christian response to human rights abuse.

TRY YOUR SKILL AT THIS

The (d) question:

'Human rights abuses only happen abroad and there is nothing we can do about it.'

In your answer you should refer to Christianity.

(i) Do you agree? Give reasons for your opinion. (3)

(ii) Give reasons why some people may disagree with you. (3)

Activity 4

Why does Archbishop Tutu say that human rights are important to Christians?

In this topic you will look at the reasons why many people think it is important to take part in the democratic and electoral processes.

KEYWORDS KEYWORDS

electoral processes the ways in which voting is organized

social change the way in which society has changed and is changing (and also the possibilities for future change)

political party a group which tries to be elected into power on the basis of its policies (e.g. Labour, Conservative)

pressure group a group formed to influence government policy on a particular issue

democratic processes the ways in which all citizens can take part in government (usually through elections)

I think it is vital to take part in the **electoral processes** of this country. By voting in an election, whether it is a local council one or a general election, we get the chance to say how we want things run. I want my voice to be heard. Voting is the way to do that. I know some people say, I'm only one amongst millions in this country and so voting doesn't matter. Rubbish! Of course it matters. If nobody bothered to vote, who would land up running our country? I don't think you can complain about what the government is doing if you didn't bother to vote.

I'm particularly keen to vote because my great-great-grandmother was one of those who fought to get the vote for women. I'd hate to think she went on hunger strike and endured force-feeding for nothing, all those years ago.

Activity 1

As a group, decide what people mean when they say 'Every country gets the government it deserves'. What does this mean for people who don't bother to vote?

I voted in the last general election because everybody with the vote should. That's what living in a democratic society means; we have all got the chance to be involved in **social change**. We can play our part in creating the sort of society we want. To be honest, I'm not convinced any **political party** – Conservative, Labour or Liberal Democrat – can really do all the things they say. They have got all sorts of policies about the way they will run the country, but things often seem to end up the same. But at least in a democracy we are free to speak out for or against the government and that can influence things.

I am on my school council because I think it is important to be involved in decision making at all levels. We talk about issues that concern the whole school community like school uniform, the convenience of the buses' pick-up points, organizing charity days, that sort of thing. Okay, it's not high-level politics, but taking part matters because it does affect our lives.

A pressure group

A **pressure group** does what it says, it 'puts the squeeze' on governments or other people who influence policy decisions. It is a very gentle squeeze though, designed to draw attention to a cause which that group believes in. The cause could vary from something local, like the closure of a post office or a school, to something national, like the problems created by landfill sites, or the poor treatment of asylum seekers. Some pressure groups work at an international level, such as Amnesty International or Make Poverty History.

The 'Make Poverty History' campaign has been one of the most successful pressure groups ever. Using peaceful means, they draw international attention to the plight of the world's poor and put pressure on world governments to act before it is too late.

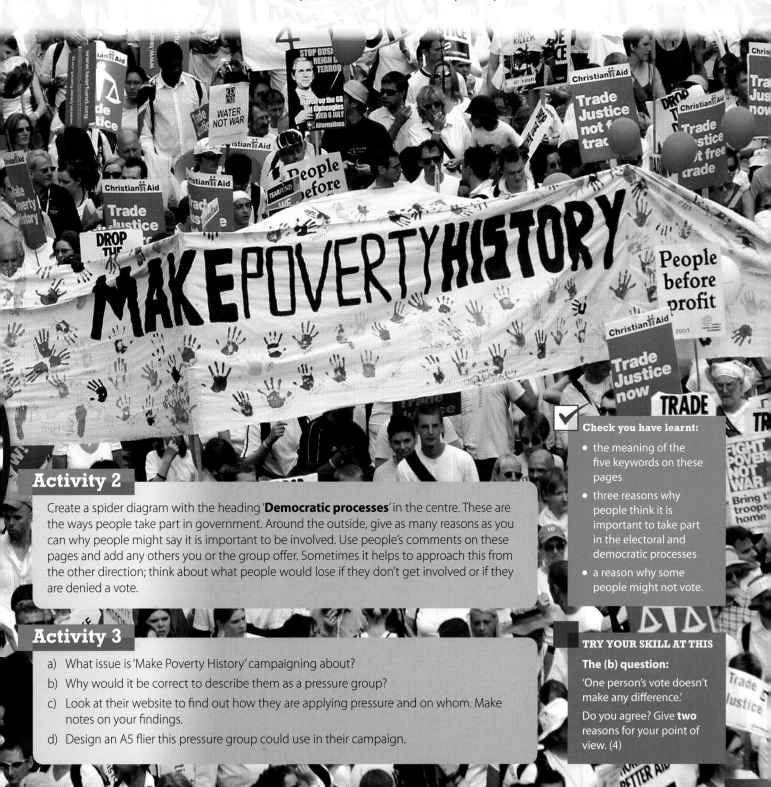

Activity 2

Create a spider diagram with the heading '**Democratic processes**' in the centre. These are the ways people take part in government. Around the outside, give as many reasons as you can why people might say it is important to be involved. Use people's comments on these pages and add any others you or the group offer. Sometimes it helps to approach this from the other direction; think about what people would lose if they don't get involved or if they are denied a vote.

Activity 3

a) What issue is 'Make Poverty History' campaigning about?

b) Why would it be correct to describe them as a pressure group?

c) Look at their website to find out how they are applying pressure and on whom. Make notes on your findings.

d) Design an A5 flier this pressure group could use in their campaign.

✓ Check you have learnt:

- the meaning of the five keywords on these pages
- three reasons why people think it is important to take part in the electoral and democratic processes
- a reason why some people might not vote.

TRY YOUR SKILL AT THIS

The (b) question:

'One person's vote doesn't make any difference.'

Do you agree? Give **two** reasons for your point of view. (4)

In this topic you will examine four Christian teachings about moral duties and responsibilities and consider their meaning.

Activity 1

How is the Golden Rule telling Christians to behave towards people they meet?

The Golden Rule

This is something you examined when studying the way Christians might approach moral decision making (page 17).

> *Do for others what you want them to do for you.*
> (Matthew 7:12)

The Parable of the Sheep and the Goats

Activity 2

Here is a story about the way people will be judged on their behaviour.

a) Who does the King represent?

b) What did the righteous people do?

c) What was the excuse given by those who didn't do good?

d) What did the King mean by: 'I tell you, whenever you did this for one of the least important of these members of my family, you did it for me.'?

e) What is this parable telling a Christian to do? And what is the reward for doing it?

> When the Son of Man comes as King and all the angels with him, he will sit on his royal throne, and the people of all nations will be gathered before him. Then he will divide them into two groups just as a shepherd separates the sheep from the goats. He will put the righteous people on his right and the others on his left. Then the King will say to the people on his right, "Come, you that are blessed by my Father! Come and possess the kingdom which has been prepared for you ever since the creation of the world. I was hungry and you fed me, thirsty and you gave me a drink; I was a stranger and you received me in your homes, naked and you clothed me; I was sick and you took care of me, in prison and you visited me."
>
> The righteous will then answer him, "When, Lord, did we ever see you hungry and feed you, or thirsty and give you a drink? When did we ever see you a stranger and welcome you in our homes, or naked and clothe you? When did we ever see you sick or in prison, and visit you?" The King will reply, **"I tell you, whenever you did this for one of the least important of these members of my family, you did it for me!"**
>
> Then he will say to those on his left, "Away from me, you that are under God's curse! Away to the eternal fire which has been prepared for the Devil and his angels! I was hungry and you would not feed me, thirsty but you would not give me a drink; I was a stranger but you would not welcome me in your homes, naked but you would not clothe me; I was sick and in prison but you would not take care of me."
>
> Then they will answer him, "When, Lord, did we ever see you hungry or thirsty or a stranger or naked or sick or in prison, and would not help you?" The King will reply, "I tell you, whenever you refused to help one of these least important ones, you refused to help me." These, then, will be sent off to eternal punishment, but the righteous will go to eternal life.
> (Matthew 24:31–46)

Am I my brother's keeper?

> *Then Adam had intercourse with his wife, and she became pregnant. She bore a son and said, "By the Lord's help I have acquired a son." So she named him Cain. Later she gave birth to another son, Abel. Abel became a shepherd, but Cain was a farmer. After some time, Cain brought some of his harvest and gave it as an offering to the Lord. Then Abel brought the first lamb born to one of his sheep, killed it, and gave the best parts of it as an offering. The Lord was pleased with Abel and his offering, but he rejected Cain and his offering. Cain became furious, and he scowled in anger. Then the Lord said to Cain, "Why are you angry? Why that scowl on your face? If you had done the right thing, you would be smiling; but because you have done evil, sin is crouching at your door. It wants to rule you, but you must overcome it."*
>
> *Then Cain said to his brother Abel, "Let's go out in the fields." When they were out in the fields, Cain turned on his brother and killed him.*
>
> *The Lord asked Cain, "Where is your brother Abel?"*
>
> *He answered, "I don't know.* **Am I supposed to take care of my brother?"**
>
> (Genesis 4:1–10)

Activity 3

Read the story of Cain and Abel.

a) What is the reply Christians would give to Cain's question at the end of this passage?

b) What would be the reason a Christian would give?

 ③

When Cain was asked what had happened to his brother, he responded by saying, 'Am I supposed to take care of my brother?' If someone asked you whether you would 'look out' for a close relative, it is likely you would say 'yes'. Most people do accept responsibility for another family member and they usually accept responsibility for you. What Christians understand from this story is that people have a responsibility for the welfare of everybody. We are all human and fellow beings on the earth.

Love one another ④

> *The message you heard from the very beginning is this: we must love one another. We must not be like Cain; he belonged to the Evil One and murdered his own brother Abel. Why did Cain murder him? Because the things he himself did were wrong, but the things his brother did were right.*
>
> *So do not be surprised, my brothers and sisters, if the people of the world hate you. We know that we have left death and come over into life; we know it because we love our brothers and sisters. Whoever does not love is still under the power of death. All who hate others are murderers, and you know that murderers have not got eternal life in them. This is how we know what love is: Christ gave his life for us. We too, then, ought to give our lives for our brothers and sisters! Rich people who see a brother or sister in need, yet close their hearts against them, cannot claim that they love God. My children, our love should not be just words and talk; it must be true love, which shows itself in action.*
>
> (1 John 3:11–18)

Activity 4

Read the 'Love one another' passage.

a) Why does this passage tell Christians that they have a duty to help a needy brother or sister?

b) Who do you think a Christian would say was their brother?

c) How can Christian love be shown?

✓ **Check you have learnt:**

- what the Golden Rule is and what it means for Christians
- two reasons why a Christian has a duty to help a needy person.

TRY YOUR SKILL AT THIS

The (d) question:

'If everyone treated others as they would like to be treated, we wouldn't need laws.'

In your answer you should refer to Christianity.

(i) Do you agree? Give reasons for your opinion. (3)

(ii) Give reasons why some people may disagree with you. (3)

DO YOU KNOW?

The (a) question

Check your knowledge of these new **KEYWORDS** you have learnt:

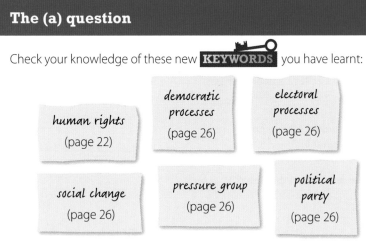

human rights (page 22)

democratic processes (page 26)

electoral processes (page 26)

social change (page 26)

pressure group (page 26)

political party (page 26)

✳ TRY THIS ✳
Practise writing out the meaning of each keyword exactly as it is given in this textbook. Learn it by heart, so you can recite it to your partner.

Now check your answers according to the mark scheme:

Partly correct answer.	1 mark
Correct answer.	2 marks

The (c) question

This question carries the most marks on the paper – **8 marks**.

Here is a typical question you might expect to see on the exam paper:

> **Explain why Christians think human rights are important.** (8)

This is how the examiner will be looking to reward your (c) answer:

Level 1	● One brief reason. ● Not explaining but describing the issue.	1–2 marks
Level 2	● Two brief reasons. ● One expanded reason.	3–4 marks
Level 3	● Three brief reasons. ● One fully-developed reason. ● Two reasons with one expanded.	5–6 marks
Level 4	● Four brief reasons. ● Two expanded reasons. ● Three reasons with one expanded.	7–8 marks

Try your skill at answering the (c) question above. Concentrate on giving as many reasons as you can and developing your points fully. When you have checked it through, look at the marking grid and decide what level you have achieved.

A tip:
The (c) question tests your understanding of the material. It does not ask for your views, so read through your answer to check how you have answered it.

WHAT DO YOU THINK?

The (b) question

Here is a typical (b) question which asks for your opinion and **two** reasons to support it.

> 'General elections are a waste of time.'
> Do you agree? Give **two** reasons for your point of view. (4)

This is how the examiner will be looking to reward your (b) answer:

Level 1	• Your opinion + brief reason.	1 mark
Level 2	• Your opinion + two brief reasons. • Your opinion + one expanded reason.	2 marks
Level 3	• Your opinion + one brief and one expanded reason.	3 marks
Level 4	• Your opinion + two expanded reasons.	4 marks

Try your skill at the (b) question above. Concentrate on giving **two** reasons. Then look at the marking grid to see how well you did.

The (d) question

Here, you are asked what you think about something and then what people who disagree with you think. A typical sort of question you might see would be:

> 'The Golden Rule only applies to Christians.'
> In your answer you should refer to Christianity.
> (i) Do you agree? Give reasons for your opinion. (3)
> (ii) Explain why some people may disagree with you. (3)

This is how the examiner will be looking to reward your (d) answer for both parts (i) and (ii):

Level 1	• One brief reason.	1 mark
Level 2	• Two brief reasons. • One expanded reason.	2 marks
Level 3	• Three brief reasons. • Two expanded reasons. • One fully-developed reason.	3 marks

This grid shows you that it's worth giving at least **two** reasons to support your view, and the more you can explain them the better.

Remember: Because this is a Religious Studies paper, you have to include what Christians think about the issues in Chapter 1. It may be that you share the same view and so it would be covered in part (i), or you may disagree with their view and put their opinion in part (ii). Either way, you must tell the examiner that *'A Christian would say … .'* or *'A Christian would agree/disagree with me because … .'*

The mark scheme says that candidates who do not refer to at least **one** religion in either part (i) or (ii) cannot go beyond 3 marks for the whole of the (d) question. Therefore, this would seriously reduce your marks. Chapter 1 *Rights and responsibilities* is based on Christianity only.

1.10 Is this the work of Frankenstein?

In this topic you will examine the nature of genetic engineering, and cloning in particular.

Activity 1

For discussion: 'Parents should be allowed to keep a frozen cloned embryo of their child. If necessary, it could be grown for use in spare-part surgery or even replace a child that might die.' Is this a horrific idea or just practical?

Activity 2

a) How was genetic engineering used in the novel and film *Jurassic Park*?

b) Use the Internet to see whether this form of 'science fiction' is possible today, and report your findings to the class.

Cloning is one idea that terrifies many people because of the possibility of creating duplicate humans.

What is genetic engineering?

This is a modern scientific process where DNA from one life form is taken out, altered and then replaced to continue growing. This can happen to a plant or an animal. People have been particularly concerned when genetic material from a totally different life form like a plant is introduced into an animal. It is possible to put the genes from a spider into a pig, or even to introduce genetic material from a strawberry into the pig. Look at the glow-in-the-dark mouse on page 34.

What is cloning?

Cloning is a form of genetic engineering that produces a duplicate cell of a parent plant or animal. Cloning plants is nothing new. In fact, you have probably done it yourself by breaking a stem off, putting it in water to grow roots and then planting it. Hey presto – a genetic copy of the parent plant!

Most people are less concerned about cloning plant life than they are about cloning animal life. Animal cloning involves genetically modifying the DNA of an egg so that the animal grows to be identical to its parent. Dolly the sheep was the first cloned animal to be born and others have followed. What worries people is the possibility of cloning a human being.

DOLLY THE SHEEP

Dolly the sheep was born in Edinburgh in 1997 and made history because she was a genetic copy of her mother – in other words, a duplicate. In the experiment 430 eggs were genetically engineered, but only 277 developed into embryos. Of those, only 23 were suitable for transplanting into the mother. Dolly was the only successful birth and her life was shorter than expected. She suffered from a lung disease and had to be put to sleep at the age of six, half the average lifespan of a sheep. Her body had aged more quickly than normal. Dolly is important because scientists proved that cloning an animal was possible.

Activity 3

Create a poster showing the arguments for and against genetic engineering.

✓ **Check you have learnt:**
- what is meant by genetic engineering
- what is meant by cloning
- two arguments in favour of genetic engineering
- two arguments against genetic engineering.

TRY YOUR SKILL AT THIS

The (b) question:

'Genetic engineering is far too dangerous for humans to experiment with.'

Do you agree? Give **two** reasons for your point of view. (4)

Is genetic engineering good or bad?

Some say it is totally wrong because scientists are manipulating the structure of living organisms. This seems like 'playing at being God' to some people. There are also questions about the long-term consequences of genetically-modified (GM) creatures. Dolly certainly had health problems. But what if these artificially-constructed life forms began breeding? Mixing the genes of plants with animal tissue is unnatural and many people think it is totally wrong.

Others say genetic engineering isn't bad in itself; what matters is how it is used. Scientists can now take damaged cells from a person, modify them to create healthy cells, and then replace them. Surely that has to be good because it will be able to offer a cure for diseases like diabetes, cystic fibrosis and many inherited medical conditions. Scientists point out that if we are going to make progress in curing diseases then genetic engineering must be permitted. Mistakes may happen along the way, but that's a small price to pay for progress.

Genetic engineering can also be used on seeds. The debate about GM maize and other crops goes on, but some people say GM crops will enable us to produce enough food to feed a hungry growing world.

What do Christians think about genetic engineering?

In this topic you will learn about the different attitudes to genetic engineering and cloning in Christianity, and the reasons for these attitudes.

This mouse was given the genes from a jellyfish to make it fluorescent. It is being used for research into treatments for cancer. Do you think this is right or wrong? Why?

Christians are divided

Genetic engineering can be looked at in two ways:

- What is going on is the manipulation of DNA, the very building blocks of life. The Bible teaches Christians that God creates life. This means it is not for humans to interfere. Some Christians say genetic engineering is 'playing God' and totally wrong. God has already decided on the genetic make-up of every life form from the outset, humans have no right to alter it. We should not be trying to make humans, or the world, perfect because only God is perfect.

- The outcome of genetic engineering can lead to good. The photographs on these pages show two ways in which genetic engineering can improve the lives of humans. Some Christians accept genetic engineering because Jesus healed people in his day and this offers a twenty-first-century form of healing. They say that if God has given us knowledge and scientific abilities, then we should use them for good.

Most Roman Catholic Christians are prepared to accept the use of genetic engineering for purposes like those shown in the photographs. But Catholics do not agree with using it on human cells. They believe only God and human parents can create a baby, and the Bible states that humans are made in God's image.

Protestants are more likely to accept genetic engineering, even that involving human cells, because they believe it is in the long-term interests of humanity. They accept the manipulation of genetic material as a form of medical research, much like drug testing, because both aim to improve people's quality of life.

Activity 1

How would you reply to the Christian who says, 'Genetic engineering is the devil's work'?

God's image under attack

CARE is a Christian charity that brings Christian insight and experience to matters of public policy and practical caring initiatives. During 2008, it put forward a Christian view of the Human Fertilization and Embryology Bill that was going before Parliament. CARE says:

"According to the Christian worldview, we are made in God's image. If we created new entities that are part human and part animal, we will distort that image and change what it means to be human. It is of huge concern."

The Methodist Church says:

"It seems that through the "engineering" or manipulation of the human genetic structure, there is a real hope of cure and relief for some very nasty and up till now incurable diseases and disabilities such as cystic fibrosis and muscular dystrophy …

Jesus of Nazareth was a healer. He cured diseases, and showed that God's purposes included overcoming "those things in his creation that spoil it and that diminish the life of his children". Clearly, where genetic manipulation is the means of healing diseases – in animals or humans – it is to be welcomed. But the dangers of it falling into the wrong hands and being used for evil ends are obvious."

Making a Christian difference for the sake of the future

Activity 2

Visit CARE's website to find out more about their concerns as Christians about genetic engineering. Write a press release they might use to tell Christians why they should be concerned.

Activity 3

Sum up the Methodist Church's attitude to genetic engineering in a paragraph. What is the Church's major concern about it?

Seed can be genetically engineered to thrive in difficult conditions. This could be a great help in the developing world where soil and climate often make agriculture challenging. Many people could be saved from starvation.

☑ **Check you have learnt:**

- two reasons why some Christians would not agree with genetic engineering
- two reasons why some Christians would permit genetic engineering.

TRY YOUR SKILL AT THIS

The (c) question:

Explain why some Christians agree with genetic engineering and some do not. (8)

SKILLS COACHING 3

END OF CHAPTER 1 CHECK

Check the (a) question

In this chapter about *Rights and responsibilities,* you will have learnt these :

Bible

Church

conscience

the Decalogue

democratic processes

electoral processes

the Golden Rule

human rights

political party

pressure group

Situation Ethics

social change

a) Choose three keywords from the list and explain what they mean.

b) Which three keywords did you not want to choose? Write down what you think their meanings might be and then check them. Or, if you really don't know, then look them up in the chapter and write down their meanings. It's better to face the difficult keywords now!

Check the (c) question

Make sure that you understand:

- the sort of authority that Christians use when making moral decisions
- the reason why human rights are important and why people should take part in democratic and electoral processes
- what is meant by genetic engineering and cloning and the different attitudes Christians have to this and their reasons.

Check the (b) and (d) questions

Check you know different people's responses to the issues above for the (b) and (d) questions.

Remind yourself of the two or three reasons the other side gives to argue against you.

Obviously, your responses to the issues above are the more important ones. Rehearse two or three reasons you would give to support your viewpoint on each issue.

Finally, the vitally important thing, what Christian viewpoint are you going to use for each issue?

Here is a typical example of how questions about *Rights and responsibilities* might be presented on the exam paper. Choose one of these questions to work through in exam conditions in order to check your progress.

SECTION 1 – RIGHTS AND REPONSIBILITIES
You must answer ONE question from this section.

EITHER

1 (a) What is **Situation Ethics**? (2)

   (b) Do you think pressure groups should be made illegal?
      Give **two** reasons for your point of view. (4)

   (c) Explain how the Bible is used by Christians in moral
      decision making. (8)

   (d) 'No good can come from genetic engineering.'
      In your answer you should refer to Christianity.
      (i) Do you agree? Give reasons for your opinion. (3)
      (ii) Give reasons why some people may disagree with you. (3)

                       (Total for Question 1 = 20 marks)

OR

2 (a) What are **democratic processes**? (2)

   (b) Do you think Christians should accept cloning?
      Give **two** reasons for your point of view. (4)

   (c) Explain why human rights matter to Christians. (8)

   (d) 'Conscience is the best guide a Christian has when making a
      moral decision.'
      In your answer you should refer to Christianity.
      (i) Do you agree? Give reasons for your opinion. (3)
      (ii) Give reasons why some people may disagree with you. (3)

                       (Total for Question 2 = 20 marks)

If this had been the real exam, how well would you have done? Use the marking grid to check your progress. Answers to (a) appear on page 9, the grid for (b) is on page 31, the grid for (c) is on page 30 and the grid for (d) is on page 31.

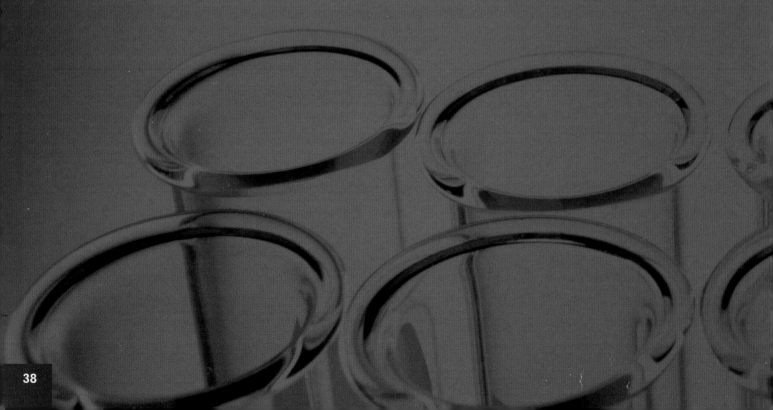

CHAPTER 2 Environmental and medical issues

artificial insemination injecting semen into the uterus by artificial means

conservation protecting and preserving natural resources and the environment

creation the act of creating the universe or the universe which has been created

embryo a fertilized egg in the first eight weeks after conception

environment the surroundings in which plants and animals live and on which they depend to live

global warming the increase in the temperature of the earth's atmosphere (thought to be caused by the greenhouse effect)

infertility not being able to have children

in-vitro fertilization the method of fertilizing a human egg in a test tube

natural resources naturally occurring materials, such as oil and fertile land, which can be used by humans

organ donation giving organs to be used in transplant surgery

stewardship looking after something so it can be passed on to the next generation

surrogacy an arrangement whereby a woman bears a child on behalf of another woman

Global warming

In this topic you will study the causes of global warming and possible solutions.

Several groups, like Greenpeace, are concerned about the way we treat the **environment**, the surroundings in which plants and animals live and upon which we all depend for our existence. One particular area they are campaigning about is climate change and the way it is causing **global warming**. Global warming is the name given to the temperature increases on earth that result from human activity. Some people also call it the greenhouse effect because the gases created from burning coal, oil and gas form a covering around the earth, just like the glass of a greenhouse. The result is an increase in the temperature of the planet.

Is this good?

When we experience a hot summer, people sometimes joke about the benefits of global warming. There is also the prospect that we will be able to grow more grapes and olives and plants that like a warmer climate. However, the picture below shows one of the less attractive sides to global warming.

Flooding like this in a small market town was caused by extreme weather in the summer of 2007. It happened again the following year. Could this be a result of global warming? Whilst we get upset seeing photographs of polar bears standing on shrinking ice flows, situations like this bring the problems of climate change very close to home!

Read what Greenpeace say about climate change:

GREENPEACE

The world is warming up. Already 150,000 people are dying every year because of climate change and, within 50 years, one-third of all land-based species could face extinction. If we carry on the way we are now, by 2100 the planet will likely be hotter than it's been at any point in the past two million years.

The impact of global warming

Glaciers, permafrost and sea ice are disappearing. Sea levels are rising, seasons changing and extreme weather becoming more extreme. As temperatures increase further, there will almost inevitably be more flooding, more drought, more diseases, more famine and more war, creating hundreds of millions of refugees and causing the destruction of entire ecosystems and species.

Activity 1

a) List all the problems Greenpeace say will result from global warming.

b) Some of the problems are linked. Draw a diagram showing the link between some of these causes and the threat to human survival.

What is causing global warming?

Greenpeace say:

"We know that climate change is caused by burning fossil fuels … For all the technological gloss of the twenty-first century, the UK is still living in an industrial era, pumping out emissions from coal, oil and gas. Worse, our energy is supplied through a criminally wasteful, centralized energy system."

- Vehicles in the UK are pumping out more greenhouse gases than ever before. Transport is responsible for 22 per cent of UK carbon emissions.
- Aviation is the fastest growing cause of climate change in the world.
- Two-thirds of all energy generated in UK power stations is lost as waste heat through chimneys and cooling towers.

Activity 2

Read through the causes of global warming. Do you think this a matter for governments to sort out or can ordinary people make a difference? Discuss in pairs or as a class.

Any solutions to global warming?

Although it sounds all doom and gloom, Greenpeace say "the good news is that we know exactly what needs to be done to stop climate change".

- Investment in renewable technology, like wind and wave power, to generate power would cut the UK's carbon emissions.
- Development of low-carbon cars.
- Reducing air travel.
- Reducing the use of fossil fuels and rainforest destruction.
- Using energy-efficient light bulbs, etc.

Activity 3

Produce a flier to go on supermarket checkouts explaining why global warming is a problem, and why reusing a plastic carrier bag is a part of the solution.

Activity 4

Create a poster to show the causes of global warming and some possible solutions.

OPERATION NOAH
Faith-motivated. Science-informed. Hope-driven.

Some Christians formed Operation Noah to fight global warming. They say, 'Climate change is the most serious environmental problem facing us today. The fate of life on earth could be decided by the choices we make in the next ten years.' What choices do you think we have?

✓ **Check you have learnt:**
- why global warming is a problem
- three factors that cause global warming
- three possible solutions.

TRY YOUR SKILL AT THIS

The (b) question:
Friends of the Earth say, 'Global climate change is the single biggest environmental threat facing the planet.' Do you agree with them? Give **two** reasons for your point of view. (4)

What's the problem?

Living on the planet creates waste. It always has done but, today, the population is very large and doubling itself ever more quickly. This means that the amount of waste we create has grown and the pressure on the environment is greater. What has also changed dramatically is the type of waste we create with our industrialized lifestyle. Modern waste no longer decays naturally, but pollutes the world we live in. These pages show just a few examples of land, sea and air pollution.

Land pollution

- 25 million tonnes of rubbish a year are dumped on streets and verges.
- UK offices produce 15 million tonnes of paper waste a year.
- Burning rubbish creates toxic ash. In landfill sites this ash emits toxic gases.
- 900,000 tonnes of electrical and electronic waste is created every year. Ninety per cent goes into landfill sites and is responsible for forty per cent of the lead found in landfill sites. Some gets into water supplies.
- Every person in the UK throws away four times their body weight in rubbish a year.

Sea pollution

- Chemical pollution from factories gets into the seas and into the food chain of polar bears, causing them to become sterile.
- Polar bears are also threatened by the effects of global warming.
- One million seabirds are killed every year by discarded plastic waste.
- Eight million pieces of litter (some plastic) go into the ocean every day.

- Eighty per cent of sea pollution comes from land-based activities.
- Raw sewage and radioactive waste have been discharged into the sea.

Air pollution

- Poor quality air is thought to result in more than 32,000 premature deaths in the UK each year.
- Petrol and diesel-engined vehicles emit a variety of pollutants into the air, including carbon monoxide, nitrogen oxides and hydrocarbons.
- Burning fossil fuels, especially coal and oil, is a major cause of air pollution. Power stations release high levels of sulphur dioxide into the atmosphere. Power stations generate electricity for industrial purposes and also for all our everyday domestic power.
- Air pollution includes the formulation of the ozone layer, smog and pollutants that lead to acid rain.
- Air pollution can cause damage to people's lungs, give people breathing problems and nose and throat irritations. It can also make existing medical conditions, such as asthma, worse.

What's the solution?

It might seem daunting, but you can:

- recycle
- buy fairtrade goods. They are made by independent farmers whose small-scale industries are much less damaging to the environment than large-scale intensive farming.
- think before you buy. Do you really need it? Avoid lots of packaging.

Activity 1

a) List **eight** ways in which humans are polluting the environment.

b) Against each point, write whether anything could realistically be done to limit the damage. List the possible solutions.

c) Add **two** further ways people could reduce pollution.

Activity 2

List three things you can personally do to reduce pollution.

 Check you have learnt:

- what is meant by pollution
- three examples of pollution
- three possible solutions for that pollution.

TRY YOUR SKILL AT THIS

The (c) question:

Explain why pollution is a major problem and what can be done about it. (8)

In this topic you will look at the scarcity of natural resources and how this poses a threat to the future of the planet. Then you will consider what possible solutions there are.

With our ever-growing population and sophisticated lifestyles, we are using up the earth's **natural resources** at an alarming rate. Natural resources are the plants, animals and minerals that occur naturally on the earth; things like trees, coal and oil. As you can see from two examples on these pages, there is a real fear that things may be reaching a stage where the earth will not be able to recover. Doing nothing about it is not an option.

I want, I get!

We have been accused of treating the planet like a giant supermarket. People with money just grab everything they want. Those who can't afford it, such as people in the developing world, go without. Worse than that, they are often left staring at the 'empty shelf' where things from their country used to be.

Activity 1

Draw a cartoon, or create a collage with magazine pictures, representing the idea in the paragraph headed 'I want, I get!' Add labels or a caption in order to get the message across.

25% of the world's population consumes 80% of the world's resources.

Activity 2

a) What is this headline actually saying? Why is this a problem?

b) Suggest **two** things we could do (no matter how small) that could work to change this.

Overfishing

The UN has expressed concern about the way the oceans are being exploited with no thought for the future. The UN said things were 'rapidly passing the point of no return' because between 71 and 78 per cent of the world's fisheries are now so depleted that many species are on the verge of extinction due to commercial fishing.

This could have an impact not just on our plate but throughout the whole balance of the marine ecosystem.

Part of the problem is that commercial fishing uses nets that kill other sea life as well.

For every tonne of prawns caught, three tonnes of other fish are killed and thrown away.

Twenty thousand porpoises die annually because they get caught up in salmon nets in the Atlantic and Pacific. Tens of thousands of dolphins are also killed annually in the tuna fishing process.

Around 2000 trees per minute are cut down in the rainforests, but it takes 60 years for a tropical rainforest tree to grow large enough for timber. The dilemma is that land is needed for increased agriculture and living space, whilst we in the West import timber for furniture. The rainforests support a complicated ecosystem and play a vital part in the way the world's climate functions.

Activity 3

With help from the Geography department, research and write a short presentation about the destruction of the rainforest. Make sure that you present both sides of the argument and explain what steps are being taken to solve the problem.

Check you have learnt:

- three natural resources that are being used up
- what is being done to conserve them
- why conservation matters for the future of the planet.

Sustainable living

The speed at which natural resources are being used up worries many people. It is a difficult balancing act. On the one hand, we need these resources to live yet, on the other hand, if humans use them, there will be nothing for future generations. One solution is to use and replace as many natural resources as possible. This is called sustainable living. When trees are cut down for fuel or furniture, then others are planted to replace them. If we recycle things we no longer want, new objects can be made from them. Using wind and wave power to create electricity is another sustainable way of living because it conserves natural resources like coal and oil.

Conservation

Some people work to protect and preserve the natural world. There is **conservation** work going on to protect the ocean's fishing stock. International governments have imposed quotas on the number of fish a country can take and also the types of nets used.

TRY YOUR SKILL AT THIS

The (b) question:

'Conservation is only for those with the time and money to spend.'

Do you agree? Give **two** reasons for your point of view. (4)

In this topic you will study the Christian teachings on stewardship and their effects on Christian attitudes to the environment.

Are there any biblical teachings about caring for the environment?

Most Christians think that there are if they interpret what is written down. In the first book of the Bible, it says:

> Then the Lord God placed the man in the Garden of Eden to cultivate it and guard it.
> **(Genesis 2:15)**

Christians believe that this means they have a responsibility to care for the environment and this idea is backed up by rules further on in the Old Testament. For instance, it says working animals must be allowed to rest every seventh day; fruit trees are not to be destroyed when attacking a city; land must be rested every seventh year, and there are many more references.

> God looked at everything he had made, and he was very pleased. **(Genesis 1:31)**

This passage tells Christians that the planet's real owner is God and we should never do anything to destroy God's **creation**.

Jesus did not actually teach about environmental issues, but that's not surprising. Two thousand years ago people lived much simpler lives that did little harm to the earth. However, Christians interpret Jesus' Sermon on the Mount to mean that they must share the earth's resources fairly.

Christians also believe that Jesus' Parable of the Gold Coins (Luke 19:11–28) teaches that they have a responsibility to hand the earth on to the next generation in a better state than they found it.

On the Day of Judgement, some Christians believe that they will be judged on the way they have treated God's created world, as well as how they have treated their fellow humans.

Activity 1

Read the Sermon on the Mount in Matthew 5:3–11 and find two teachings that could lead Christians to understand that they must share resources fairly.

Activity 2

Explain why the Parable of the Gold Coins could be connected with stewardship.

Being a good steward

Christians believe that we do not own the planet. God the creator owns the planet, he loans it to humans to use in their lifetime. At the end of time, the earth must be returned to its rightful owner in good condition. Christians use the term **stewardship** for this. You might think of a person as being like an air steward who can use whatever is necessary for the passengers' comfort during their flight. But the owners of the airline do not expect anything to be wasted or destroyed by their stewards, and at the end of the shift things have to be left in good order ready for the next crew to take over.

For Christians, stewardship means that they should not exploit the planet by harming it or wasting its resources. People should work in harmony with creation rather than against it.

Activity 3

With a partner, discuss what problems the next generation might have with the state of the planet if we do nothing. Decide on **two** ways in which people could improve the planet they are handing on.

What effect do these teachings have on Christians?

Some Christians are more environmentally aware than others, but most believe that they should do their best to protect the environment. Some recycle and try to reduce their carbon footprint.

Others approach it in a different way, focusing on their responsibility to share the earth's resources more fairly amongst its inhabitants. Charities like Christian Aid work to put this into practice by helping people in the developing world make a sustainable way of living for themselves. Not all Christians can do this kind of work, but many choose to support it by giving money.

Activity 4

'If the earth was a present from God, then we can use it as we like.'

How would a Christian respond to this statement?

This is one project this group of Christians is working on to put stewardship into practice. Look at A Rocha's website to see some other ways.

INTERNATIONAL A ROCHA NEWS

Christians in Conservation - Issue 45 - October 2008

Help to save Tana River Delta!

African Fish Eagle *Haliaeetus vocifer*
Photos: © Cheryl-Samantha Owen

Two huge new sugar plantations are being planned for the north Kenya coast, as well as new sugar factories and bio-fuel plants which will have massively damaging environmental and social impacts. The project threatens to destroy one of the biggest freshwater wetlands in Kenya: the Tana River Delta. The large local community, primarily pastoralists whose culture has evolved around the seasonal ebb and flow of the wetlands, is campaigning hard to save their way of life.

A Rocha Kenya is taking part in the campaign

A Rocha Kenya is working closely with other conservation organisations, particularly NatureKenya, the Kenya Wetlands Forum and the East African Wildlife Society. The A Rocha team is also making two distinctive contributions:

1. Sharing bird count data

2. Managing the Tana River Delta website

☑ Check you have learnt:

- the meaning of Christian stewardship
- three Christian teachings that lead Christians to care for the earth
- three ways stewardship can be put into practice.

TRY YOUR SKILL AT THIS

The (d) question:

'Religion is about prayer, not the environment.'

In your answer you should refer to at least one religion.

(i) Do you agree? Give reasons for your opinion. (3)

(ii) Give reasons why some people may disagree with you. (3)

Activity 5

Read the article about A Rocha – a Christian environmental organization – and the work they are doing in Kenya.

a) What environmental problems are involved?

b) What are A Rocha doing to help?

c) What religious reasons might they give for their work?

In this topic you will study the Muslim teachings on stewardship and their effects on Muslim attitudes to the environment.

Muslim Declaration on Nature

We are God's stewards and agents on earth. We are not masters of this earth: it does not belong to us to do what we wish. It belongs to God and he has entrusted us with its safekeeping.

The Qur'an tells Muslims that Allah created the world and everything in it for a purpose; it is part of Allah's plan. Nothing in it is a waste of space or time. Muslims also believe that everything in existence is interlinked, we are all part of 'one'. If one life form is damaged, it upsets a link in the chain and that harms the planet.

Khalifah

Muslims believe that Allah has provided all the resources humans need to live on earth and they can use them, but people should not damage or waste these resources. Muslims use the Arabic word 'khalifah' for this idea of stewardship, and a person who acts as Allah's steward is also called a *khalifah*. The first *khalifah* was Adam. The Qur'an states: 'I am placing on the earth one who shall rule as my deputy.'

Everyone has a duty to be a *khalifah* and the way to do this is to follow the way of life set out in the Qur'an. On the Day of Judgement, Allah will judge everybody on the way they have treated his creation.

Here Prophet Muhammad explains the role of *khalifah*:

> The world is green and beautiful and Allah has appointed you his steward over it. The whole earth has been created as a place of worship pure and clean.

This group of African Muslims believes that caring for the environment will also improve the plight of the poorest people in Africa. AMEN has taught people how to revive traditional Swahili fishing trapping techniques and to sell their ecologically-harvested fish to hotels. They have also worked with women to develop organic honey production and to sell their produce through a fair trade organization.

For Muslims, being a *khalifah* also means sharing out the world's resources more fairly. This is what AMEN is working towards.

AMEN says:

"Our role is to protect and to use God's creation thoughtfully and carefully so that on the Day of Judgement we can report back to God that we have been true and faithful *khalifahs*."

This is what one Islamic environmentalist has said about our treatment of the earth's resources:

> I have a mental picture of people sharing in a massive banquet completely oblivious to the fact that the roof is crumbling and will eventually come crashing down on their heads. There are other people standing at the exits warning the diners to leave, but they don't take any notice since the meal is too good.
>
> (Mr Khalid)

Putting stewardship into action

LINE stands for London Islamic Network for the Environment. Set up in 2004, it is the UK's first local Islamic environmental group.

LINE provides a monthly forum for people to meet and discuss environmental issues. They have campaigned to draw attention to environmental problems and solutions.

LINE also organizes outings to provide people with the opportunity to connect with nature.

Their regular newsletter has articles which have included helpful tips such as:

- asking readers to consider walking or taking public transport to attend Friday prayers, rather than driving to the mosque;
- encouraging readers to buy local, organic food rather than supermarket products, in order to protect the environment and to support local businesses;
- asking readers to think about whether they really need something before buying it, following the advice in the Qur'an:

 But waste not by excess: for God loves not the wasters. **(6:141)**

Activity 2

Either:

Explain the connection Mr Khalid is making between a lot of people feasting and the way we treat the planet.

Or:

Draw a cartoon of the image described and add labels to explain the point.

Activity 3

Prepare material for a web page for the internet site 'Green Islam' suggesting **three** ways Muslims could be *khalifahs*.

Members of LINE dressed in snorkels and flippers to highlight the threat of floods in Bangladesh from rising sea levels due to climate change.

 Check you have learnt:

- what is meant by *khalifah*
- two reasons why Muslims should care for the environment
- how some Muslims put stewardship into action.

Participants get involved in a LINE tree-planting day in an organic farm in Oxfordshire.

TRY YOUR SKILL AT THIS

The (c) question:

Choose **one** *religion other than Christianity* and explain why its followers have a responsibility to care for the environment?

Give **two** reasons for your point of view. (4)

SKILLS COACHING 4

DO YOU KNOW?

Improve your skill with the (a) question

In this chapter so far, you have learnt six **KEYWORDS**:

> environment
> (page 40)

> global warming
> (page 40)

> conservation
> (page 42)

> natural resources
> (page 42)

> creation
> (page 46)

> stewardship
> (page 46)

✳ TRY THIS ✳
Write down the definition of each keyword without checking back. Then look the words up to see if you got them right.

The best way to be certain of your 2 marks every time is to learn the exact definition that is given. Can you recite it word for word? Don't worry if you can't manage it, other wording is acceptable so long as it means exactly the same thing.

Improve your skill with the (c) question

Here is an example of a typical question:

Explain why the scarcity of natural resources is a big concern and what could be done about this. **(8)**

STEP 1

Copy the question down on your page and underline the important words. Your version may well look like this:

Explain why the scarcity of natural resources is a big concern and what could be done about this.

STEP 2

Draw a line down your page and head the first column 'A big concern' and the second 'What can be done?' Note down as many points as you can in each column. Look back in the textbook to help you. Aim to put three points in each column.

STEP 3

Write up the notes you have made in full sentences, one sentence for each point.

Start your first paragraph *'Some people believe the scarcity of natural resources is a big concern because …'.* Then begin a new paragraph *'Some of the things that could be done about this are …'.*

Use the mark scheme on page 30 to mark your answer. How did you do?

WHAT DO YOU THINK?

Improve your skill with the (b) question

This question asks for your opinion. Here are the sort of things you could be asked about:

Do you think being 'green' is the most important thing in the world?

Do religious people have a greater responsibility for the earth than anyone else?

Is global warming the biggest problem facing the planet?

Do you think the environment is really a religious issue?

Give **two** reasons for your point of view. (4)

Choose **one** of the (b) questions to work on.

STEP 3

To get the full 4 marks for the (b) question, you need to develop each point into a reasoned sentence. So you could write:

I don't think religion is about environmental things really. It's to do with spiritual things like contacting God. Religious people should read the scriptures and try to lead the sort of life God wants them to. ✓ 2 marks

Another reason is that the environment concerns everybody. We all live here and if we don't care for it we will all suffer. ✓ 2 marks

STEP 2

Now note down **two** reasons you would give. If your reasons are just brief comments, you will only gain 2 marks. For example, if you chose the question that asks '**Do you think the environment is really a religious issue?**' you might decide 'no' and jot down that the religion is just about contacting God ✓ 1 mark and everybody ought to care about the environment. ✓ 1 mark

But those answers are a bit brief, aren't they?

STEP 1

Decide whether your response is going to be 'Yes' or 'No'. There are no marks for saying this, but it is important to be clear in your own mind what view you are going to take.

☑ Choose a different question to answer. When you have completed it, swap answers with a partner and award marks according to the mark scheme on page 31.

What can be done if someone isn't able to have children?

In this topic you will study the nature and importance of medical treatments for infertility.

KEYWORDS KEYWORD

infertility not being able to have children

artificial insemination injecting semen into the uterus by artificial means

in-vitro fertilization the method of fertilizing a human egg in a test tube

embryo a fertilized egg in the first eight weeks after conception

surrogacy an arrangement whereby a woman bears a child on behalf of another woman

Activity 1

For discussion: Do you think everybody has the right to have a child?

Points to consider:

- The age of the couple, particularly the mother.
- The type of relationship a child might be born into: heterosexual/ homosexual/single parent.
- The cost of fertility treatment to the NHS.

Keep notes of the discussion because these points are useful for revision.

Many people's greatest wish is to be able to have children.

What if a couple fail to conceive a child?

There comes a point in many people's lives when they want to have children. It often seems a natural stage in a couple's relationship and, added to that, the survival of the human race depends on it! Many women feel an emotional need to have a baby and can suffer deep unhappiness if there are problems. However, what medical treatment is available for those who want to have a child but are **infertile**?

Louise Brown, born in 1978, was the first 'test-tube baby'. Her conception was the result of IVF. Today, 6000 babies are born every year in the UK as a result of IVF.

Artificial insemination by husband, known as AIH – sperm is taken from the husband and placed in the woman's uterus. This can help couples who have difficulty conceiving for no obvious reason.

In-vitro fertilization, known as IVF – egg and sperm are taken from a couple, fertilized in a laboratory and then placed in the womb. This helps women with medical problems, such as blocked fallopian tubes, to conceive.

Artificial insemination by donor, known as AID – sperm donated to a clinic by a man is placed in a woman's uterus. This can help couples where the man is infertile.

Egg donation – a fertilized egg is created in the laboratory using an egg donated by another woman but using the partner's sperm. The fertilized egg is placed in the woman's womb. This is of help when a woman does not ovulate.

Embryo donation – a donated egg and donated sperm are fertilized in the laboratory to form an **embryo** before being placed in a woman's womb.

What options are available to infertile couples?

Surrogacy – a woman (the surrogate mother) agrees to become pregnant with someone else's child and then hand that child over after it is born. This can be achieved with IVF using the couple's sperm and egg and planting the fertilized embryo in the surrogate mother. A surrogate mother may also permit her egg to be fertilized by having sperm from the father inserted into her uterus. Although surrogacy is controversial, it is legal in the UK provided the surrogate mother does it purely to help a couple and not as a paid job.

Activity 2

Use the BBC News website, or an online newspaper, to discover what Parliament discussed about fertility treatment in 2008. What decisions were made about experiments using mixed human and animal embryos? Discuss your findings in the group.

✓ Check you have learnt:

- what is meant by infertility
- reasons why people believe treating infertility is important
- six medical treatments available for infertility.

Activity 3

Write a letter from Sophie to her doctor explaining why it is important to her to receive fertility treatment on the NHS.

TRY YOUR SKILL AT THIS

The (b) question:

Do you think fertility treatment should be available to everybody on the NHS?

Give **two** reasons for your point of view. (4)

Who decides what is legal?

The Human Fertilization and Embryology Authority (HFEA) regulates medical treatments for infertility in the UK and its work is governed by the Human Fertilization and Embryology Act of 1990, which was reviewed in 2008. Any individual cases that are unclear ask the courts for guidance.

In this topic you will learn about the different attitudes to infertility treatments among Christians and the reasons for those attitudes.

Activity 1

If children are a gift from God, why might this lead some Christians to be against fertility treatment?

Christians agree that having a child is important for a married couple because it creates a family. This is stated in the marriage ceremony and a child is seen as a gift from God. Roman Catholics and Protestants differ in the way they approach the issue of infertility treatment.

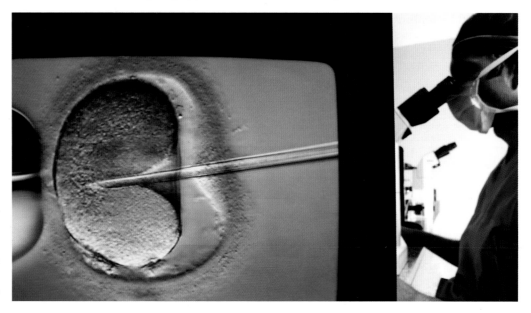

An egg that has been taken from a woman is being fertilized in the laboratory. Why might some Christians disagree with this procedure?

What is the Roman Catholic attitude to fertility treatment?

Catholics understand that a child is God's gift to a couple, conceived as a result of a loving sexual relationship between a husband and wife. Anything else is unnatural and not what God intended. This means Catholics do not accept any fertilization treatments involving artificial manipulation of an egg or sperm in a laboratory.

There are other reasons why Catholics think artificial fertility treatment is wrong. The IVF process involves the creation of several fertilized eggs. Not all the eggs will be implanted in the woman, the rest will be destroyed. Catholics believe it is wrong to destroy human life after the moment of conception. In addition, all forms of artificial insemination require sperm to be produced by masturbation, which is a sin for Catholics.

Because the Catholic Church believes children are a vital part of a marriage, there are Catholic doctors at medical centres like the Pope Paul VI Institute who can offer help to couples having difficulty conceiving. This institute opened in 1985 to study natural fertility and reproductive medicine. It is run according to the teachings of the Catholic Church and the principle that 'love and life should never be separated'. The Church also urges infertile couples to think of adopting a child because this helps both the child and the couple.

Activity 2

Write **two** different replies to this letter, one from a Catholic priest and the other from a Church of England priest. Make sure each contains the religious reasons for their advice.

> I would love to have children but my cancer treatment left me sterile. My sister has offered to carry a child for me. Is this allowed if my husband's sperm is used?
>
> Marie

> " *Techniques that entail the dissociation of husband and wife, by the intrusion of a person other than the couple (donation of sperm or ovum, surrogate uterus), are gravely immoral. These techniques (heterologous artificial insemination and fertilization) infringe the child's right to be born of a father and mother known to him and bound to each other by marriage. They betray the spouses' "right to become a father and a mother only through each other".* "
> (Catechism of the Catholic Church 2376)

Activity 3

With a partner, work out the reasons the Catholic Church gives for refusing artificial insemination.

What do other Christians think about fertility treatment?

There is a wide difference of opinion amongst non-Catholics on the subject of fertility treatment.

- Some Evangelical Christians share the Catholic view that if a child is God's gift, then humans have no right to interfere with God's plan.

- Other Christians argue that if God gave us the knowledge and ability to help infertile couples, we should use it. The Bible contains stories of God bringing happiness to an infertile woman by giving her a child. They conclude that it is an act of great kindness to help a woman to conceive a longed-for child and remove her suffering.

- Some Christians will accept fertility treatment so long as a husband's sperm and a wife's egg are involved. Using donated egg or sperm may be regarded as a form of adultery. Others argue that it is important for a child's emotional welfare that they are genetically related to their parents.

- Some Protestants disagree with IVF because it involves the destruction of 'spare' fertilized embryos. Although these embryos are less than 14 days old, some Christians believe that they are a human life with the same status as a baby. Their destruction, or use in medical research, is wrong.

Activity 4

Make a poster showing different Christian approaches to fertility treatment.

Patricia Rashbrook is the oldest British woman to have a baby at the age of 62. In 2006, she paid £10,000 for Russian fertility treatment using a donated egg and sperm from her 60-year-old husband. Although UK law does not impose any age limit on women becoming mothers, it says doctors must take into account the welfare of the child and the ability of patients to provide a stable, healthy upbringing.

✔ **Check you have learnt:**

- two reasons why some Christians do not permit fertility treatment
- two reasons why some Christians agree with fertility treatment.

TRY YOUR SKILL AT THIS

The (c) question:

Explain why some Christians agree with fertility treatment and some do not. (8)

In this topic you will learn about the different attitudes to infertility treatments among Muslims and the reasons for those attitudes.

Islam teaches that a child is a gift from Allah. For some Muslims, this means that nobody has the right to intervene because Allah has a plan for everyone; he decides who he will give children to and who he will not. No human being can presume to know the mind of Allah and nobody should consider intervening in Allah's plan.

Other Muslims argue that every woman has the right to be a mother and medical help should be available to treat infertility. Infertility is an illness like any other, and doctors should treat a man or woman suffering from infertility.

Many Muslims regard infertility as a disease that couples are entitled to receive treatment for.

Activity 1

'Decisions about fertility treatment in Islam hinge on whether adultery is involved.'

Explain what forms of treatment would be unacceptable to a Muslim and why.

Activity 2

Create a diagram to help you revise Muslim attitudes to different fertility treatments. Put **Husband** and **Wife** in the centre, so you remain focused on the married relationship.

The type of fertility treatment that can be offered to a Muslim couple is determined by the Islamic teachings on marriage and relationships. Sexual relationships can only exist within marriage, anything else is forbidden in Islam as being adultery.

- **IVF** is acceptable to many Muslims provided that it uses the egg and sperm of the married couple themselves. Anything else is forbidden and considered as adultery. Most Muslims do not think it is wrong for the spare embryos created by IVF treatment to be destroyed. This is because Islam teaches that an embryo only becomes fully human at 120 days, when Allah breathes a soul into the embryo.

- **AIH** (artificial insemination by the husband) would also be acceptable to many Muslims.

- **AID** (artificial insemination by donor) is totally forbidden because the donor is not married to the woman. The Qur'an also makes it clear that everyone has a right to a lineage, in other words a family identity that neither AID or egg donation provide.

- **Surrogacy** is not permitted because it requires a man's sperm to be put into a woman he is not married to. Because surrogacy also upsets the idea of lineage, it would also make it a sin.

Diane Blood made legal history in 1998 when she gave birth to a baby using her dead husband's sperm. Because the sperm had been taken from her husband when he was in a coma and could not give his consent, its use was illegal under British law. However, the Court of Appeal allowed Mrs Blood to take the sperm to Europe for IVF treatment because it was known her husband had wanted them to start a family. Islam does not permit treatment like this because the egg and sperm have to come from a couple who are married. If one partner is dead, they are no longer considered married.

Who are you?

Islam says that every child has the right to an identity. This could be problem if a child was conceived using the egg or sperm of someone who was not the child's real parent. Surrogacy also raises the issue of who is the child's real mother. Is it the woman who gave birth to the child? Is it the woman whose egg was used? Is it the woman who brings the child up?

Activity 3

For discussion: Do you think it would cause a person any emotional problems if they discovered that they had been born to a surrogate mother using donated sperm and egg?

Adoption?

Muslim couples who are unable to have children are encouraged to take care of orphans or children who have been abandoned. Muhammad himself was an orphan and as an adult he took care of the orphan Zayd within his own family. Many passages in the Qur'an urge Muslims to show compassion towards orphans and explain how Allah will judge people on the compassion they showed to orphans. There is no legal adoption process in Islam because Muslims do not believe it is right for a child to be given the identity of their adoptive family.

Check you have learnt:

- reasons why some Muslims reject fertility treatment
- reasons why some Muslims accept some fertility treatments
- that any fertility treatment that involves adultery is wrong.

TRY YOUR SKILL AT THIS

The (c) question:

Explain why some Muslims accept fertility treatment and others do not. (8)

DO YOU KNOW?

Improve your skill with the (a) question

Five **KEYWORDS** have appeared in the past section. Using the exact definitions, answer the following:

What does **embryo** mean? (2)

What is meant by **infertility**? (2)

What is meant by **in-vitro fertilization**? (2)

What does **surrogacy** mean? (2)

What is meant by **artificial insemination**? (2)

Using the keywords in your answers will also gain you marks because it shows you can use specialist vocabulary.

✱ TRY THIS ✱

Here are the meanings of two keywords from earlier in Chapter 2. What are the correct keywords?

? = the increase in the temperature of the earth's atmosphere (thought to be caused by the greenhouse effect).

? = protecting and preserving natural resources and the environment.

Improve your skill with the (c) question

The (c) question is the big one because it is testing quite a few things and that is why it carries 8 marks. The examiner wants you to show that you have a good knowledge and understanding of the topic. This means you *either* need to give plenty of reasons *or* develop the examples you have given.

The question is likely to contain the word *Explain* in it. Sometimes you will be asked to *Explain why* something is the case. It may be the case, in the religion you have been studying, followers don't agree on their response to an issue. If that is the case, think about answering the question like this:

'Some think this because … .'

'But others think this because … .'

Some (c) questions may ask you for two different viewpoints, often by asking why some believers agree with an issue and why others do not. **For this type of question it is important that you give both sides of the argument.** If you can expand on the reasons you give in each case, you can move your answer up to the higher levels.

Here are some questions that might require two viewpoints:

Explain why some Christians agree with fertility treatment and others do not. (8)

Choose **one** *religion other than Christianity* and explain why some of its followers agree with artificial insemination and others do not. (8)

Explain why surrogacy is such a controversial issue. (8)

Choose **one** of the questions above and start planning it step by step as you learnt on page 20.

Question (c) will give **the QWC marks** for the exam.

■ So remember to write in paragraphs – one for each side of the argument.

■ Check that you have used full sentences and punctuated them correctly.

■ Check that you have included some specialist terms. Are there any keywords you could include?

A tip:

The (c) question is **not** asking for your opinion, so **do not** say

'I think …'.

WHAT DO YOU THINK?

Improve your skill with the (d) question

This is the opportunity for you to have your say and explain your reasons. Question (b) and question (d) are both asking for your opinion.

You have practised question (b) on page 51, so let's tackle question (d). It is similar to (b) but also tests whether you can understand someone else's point of view that is different from your own. There are 6 marks for the whole answer, with 3 given for each half of the question.

Here are some typically controversial statements about fertility treatment you might see in a (d) question:

'If God decides a couple aren't having children, no one should intervene.'

'Surrogacy can lead to all sorts of problems.'

'Everybody should be entitled to fertility treatment.'

'IVF treatment is wrong because it's interfering with nature.'

The (d) question will then go on to ask:

In your answer you should refer to at least one religion.

(i) Do you agree? Give reasons for your opinion. (3)

(ii) Give reasons why some people may disagree with you. (3)

STEP 3

Then tackle part (ii) in the same way, only this time you begin with 'Some people may disagree with me because … '. Express the points in your table as fully as possible.

STEP 2

As you did for the (b) question, start with your opinion. This time it will go in part (i). Start with 'I think …' and then go on to express as fully as you can the reasons you have listed. Look back to the mark scheme on page 31 to remind yourself of exactly what the examiner is looking for.

STEP 1

Draw two columns on your page and head one side 'Agree' and the other side 'Disagree'. Write two or three reasons in each column. Check that some of them are religious reasons and put the name of the religion against it.

A tip:

Have you included specialist terms or keywords?

Have you included a religious viewpoint and said which religion it might belong to?

In this topic you will consider the nature and importance of transplant surgery.

KEYWORDS KEYWORD

organ donation giving organs to be used in transplant surgery

Over the past 50 years, it has become routine for patients with diseased organs to be offered transplant surgery. This involves a donated organ being surgically grafted to replace the patient's own and enable them to have a better quality of life. This can vary from something small like the transplant of the cornea of an eye, to the transplant of a major organ like the heart. The first successful human heart transplant was in 1967 and caused a lot of controversy. People questioned who a person would be if they had the heart of someone else, especially when we traditionally say, 'I love you with all my heart'.

Equally as controversial, three years earlier a chimpanzee's heart had been successfully transplanted into a man.

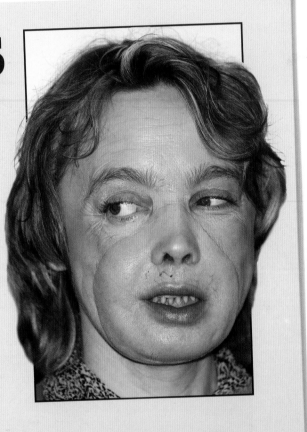

LET'S FACE IT

Isabelle Dinoire had a successful partial face transplant in 2005. When her nose, lips and chin were torn off by a dog, French surgeons realized the injuries were too severe to repair. Instead, they made medical history with the world's first facial transplant.

Dead or alive?

Obviously, organs like a heart can only come from a dead person, but some organs like kidneys can be donated by a live donor because we have two kidneys. Donor and recipient can go on to lead a healthy life. Bone marrow, which can help some cancer sufferers, can also be given by a live donor. However, as with all organ transplants, the tissue of the donor and the recipient has to be matched before surgery is considered.

Activity 1

a) Explain why some people might think there is a big difference between giving a kidney and giving a heart for transplant.

b) Would you consider giving one of your kidneys if your mum had two diseased kidneys? Why? Would you think differently about donating to somebody unknown?

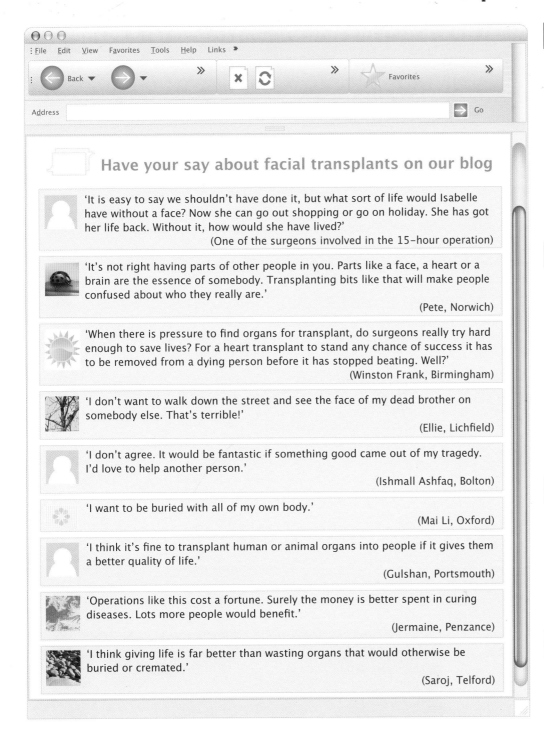

File   Edit   View   Favorites   Tools   Help   Links »

Back   Favorites

Address   Go

Have your say about facial transplants on our blog

'It is easy to say we shouldn't have done it, but what sort of life would Isabelle have without a face? Now she can go out shopping or go on holiday. She has got her life back. Without it, how would she have lived?'

(One of the surgeons involved in the 15–hour operation)

'It's not right having parts of other people in you. Parts like a face, a heart or a brain are the essence of somebody. Transplanting bits like that will make people confused about who they really are.'

(Pete, Norwich)

'When there is pressure to find organs for transplant, do surgeons really try hard enough to save lives? For a heart transplant to stand any chance of success it has to be removed from a dying person before it has stopped beating. Well?'

(Winston Frank, Birmingham)

'I don't want to walk down the street and see the face of my dead brother on somebody else. That's terrible!'

(Ellie, Lichfield)

'I don't agree. It would be fantastic if something good came out of my tragedy. I'd love to help another person.'

(Ishmall Ashfaq, Bolton)

'I want to be buried with all of my own body.'

(Mai Li, Oxford)

'I think it's fine to transplant human or animal organs into people if it gives them a better quality of life.'

(Gulshan, Portsmouth)

'Operations like this cost a fortune. Surely the money is better spent in curing diseases. Lots more people would benefit.'

(Jermaine, Penzance)

'I think giving life is far better than wasting organs that would otherwise be buried or cremated.'

(Saroj, Telford)

UK facts and figures for 2008

- 8000 people are on the transplant waiting lists in the UK.
- Numbers waiting for a transplant organ rise by 80 per cent every year.
- 3000 organ transplants are carried out each year.
- 1000 people on the waiting list die every year.
- Organs can only be taken if a person has signed the organ donor register.
- Organs can be donated if the family agrees.
- One donor can save up to nine lives, and improve 50 more through tissue donation.

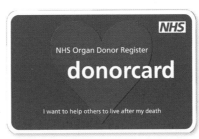

NHS

NHS Organ Donor Register

donorcard

I want to help others to live after my death

*Some people choose to carry an organ donor card. In 2008, the British government discussed and rejected changes to make **organ donation** automatic unless a person opts out.*

Activity 2

Read this email discussion resulting from Isabelle Dinoire's story. Draw two columns on your page, one headed 'In favour' and the other 'Against'. Note down the different arguments being offered on this subject.

Activity 3

Some people in less economically developed countries are paid if they donate kidneys. Some of these organs have been used for transplant surgery in the West. Should people be able to buy and sell organs? Give reasons for your opinion.

Activity 4

For discussion: Should UK hospitals have an automatic right to take a person's organs for transplant unless they have registered a refusal?

✓ Check you have learnt:

- the difference between live and dead organ donation
- three arguments in favour of transplant surgery
- three arguments against transplant surgery.

TRY YOUR SKILL AT THIS

The (b) question:

'Transplant surgery should be banned.'

Do you agree? Give **two** reasons for your point of view. (4)

What do Christians think about transplant surgery?

In this topic you will examine the different attitudes to transplant surgery in Christianity and the reasons for those attitudes.

Christians differ in their attitude to transplant surgery, although the majority accept it.

Christians who totally reject transplant organs say:

- the Bible states that humans are created by God in his image. This means people have no right to interfere with God's creation. The sanctity of life means that all life is holy and belongs to God.
- those Christians who believe that God will resurrect people in their bodies at the end of the world do not agree with transplanting organs.

Some Christians are against organs being taken from the dead for transplant surgery but would agree to using those donated by living relatives. They say:

- living organs are freely given out of love
- when we have two organs, giving one is permissible because it is following Jesus' teachings of loving your neighbour
- if an organ is donated by a relative, there is no chance poor people in less economically developed countries have been exploited.

Other Christians who accept transplant surgery of organs donated from the dead argue that:

- the gift of life is precious and it is right to make every effort to preserve life
- there are various teachings in the Bible that lead Christians to believe transplant surgery is acceptable. St Paul told his followers, 'I myself can say that you would have taken out your own eyes, if you could, and given them to me' (Galatians 4:15). Whilst such surgery was impossible in St Paul's day, Christians believe that it provides guidance on the principle of organ donation
- some Christians believe that we will be resurrected in spirit after we die, but not in body. This would mean that our body is no longer needed and they see nothing wrong in using it to help the living
- the Golden Rule teaches Christians to treat others as they would like to be treated themselves. For some, this is sufficient support for organ donation and transplant surgery
- Christianity teaches the importance of sacrifice and of helping others – organ donation is just that.

Useful specialist terms

sanctity of life the belief that life is holy and belongs to God

Activity 1

In Luke 3:11 Jesus said, 'Whoever has two shirts must give one to the man who has none, and whoever has food must share it.' What might this mean for a Christian whose uncle needs a kidney transplant?

Activity 2

a) Why would some Christians permit cornea grafting and others disagree with it?

b) Would you accept the offer of a cornea transplant if you needed one? Would you permit your corneas to be used for transplants after your death? Why?

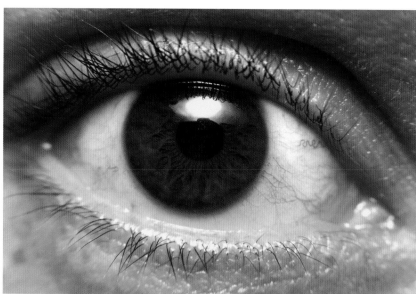

Cornea transplants are routine, approximately 100,000 are carried out annually around the world. The cornea that is grafted has been donated by somebody who has died.

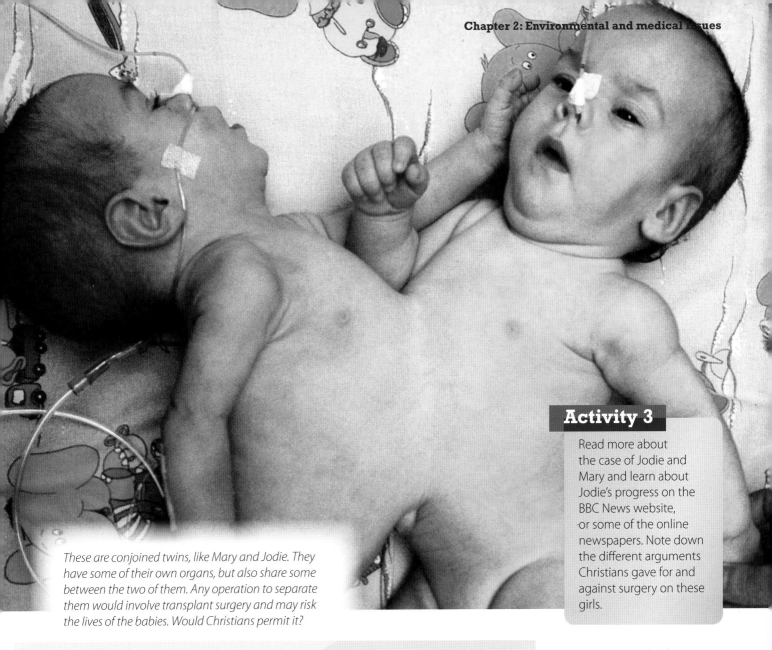

These are conjoined twins, like Mary and Jodie. They have some of their own organs, but also share some between the two of them. Any operation to separate them would involve transplant surgery and may risk the lives of the babies. Would Christians permit it?

Activity 3

Read more about the case of Jodie and Mary and learn about Jodie's progress on the BBC News website, or some of the online newspapers. Note down the different arguments Christians gave for and against surgery on these girls.

The difficult case of Jodie and Mary

Roman Catholics were faced with a difficult ethical dilemma when conjoined twins Jodie and Mary were born to Catholic parents in 2000. Mary, the weaker twin, shared many organs with her twin Jodie. If they were not separated, both twins would die because Jodie's heart and lungs were doing the work for both of them. Doctors wanted to separate the twins and transplant all the organs into Jodie so she would stand a chance of surviving. This would mean the death of Mary.

The twins' parents refused because they said that what had happened was God's will and humans should not intervene. They wanted the twins cared for but nature to be allowed to take its course even though surgeons said the twins were unlikely to survive beyond six months. A court case followed and doctors were given permission to go against the parents' wishes and separate the twins even though it was known one would die.

Alan Dickson, one of the two leading surgeons in the team of 22 who did the operation and is a committed Christian, spoke of the moment when they severed Mary's blood supply: 'It was an intense moment. We looked at each other because we knew what we were doing at the time. One doesn't do that kind of thing without having a lot of thought and a lot of heartache. The theatre was very quiet and we treated that moment with the utmost dignity and respect.' Mary died but, after further operations, Jodie has been able to enjoy a normal life.

Check you have learnt:

- three different Christian attitudes towards transplant surgery
- the reasons for these attitudes
- why the case of Jodie and Mary was controversial.

TRY YOUR SKILL AT THIS

The (c) question:

Explain why some Christians agree with transplant surgery and others do not. (8)

In this topic you will examine the different attitudes to transplant surgery in Islam and the reasons for those attitudes.

Like Christians, Muslims are divided about transplant surgery.

Those against transplant surgery

- The Qur'an teaches that on the Last Day, Allah will resurrect everybody bodily. It is understood that nothing should be removed from a person's body after death and Islam does not permit post-mortems, unless absolutely necessary.
- Teachings about the sanctity of life mean that many Muslims do not think humans should harm the body that is Allah's creation.
- Allah is the creator of life and he has a plan for everyone. Humans have no right to alter Allah's plan about life and death.

Those who are prepared to accept transplant surgery

- Islam teaches that it is every Muslim's duty to alleviate suffering and save life. Organ donation and transplants can do this.
- Organ donation from a living donor is permitted, so long as it does not risk the donor's life as a result.
- In 1995, the Muslim Council of Britain permitted Muslims to carry a donor card and have transplants.
- If a person agrees during their lifetime to donate their organs, this is an act of charity.
- There are Muslim transplant surgeons and lawyers who believe that organ donation and transplant surgery are acceptable because they can save lives.

No Muslim is permitted to sell their organs because it degrades the human body.

Activity 1

How might the following quotation from the Qur'an influence a Muslim's attitude towards organ donation and transplant surgery?

> *Does Man think that We [Allah] shall not assemble his bones? Yes, surely, yes – We are able to restore even his finger-tips.*
>
> **(Qur'an 75:3–4)**

Activity 2

Read the following extract. Write down the reasons this Muslim doctor gives for working on transplant surgery.

> *"Organ donation is the gift of life – there is no greater gift. Charity is very important within Islam and we want people to see organ donation as the greatest act of charity.*
>
> *I would not practice this profession [transplant surgery] if I did not believe it is right according to my faith."*
>
> **(Mr Aiman Alzetani MD FRCS(C-Th) Cardiothoracic surgeon)**

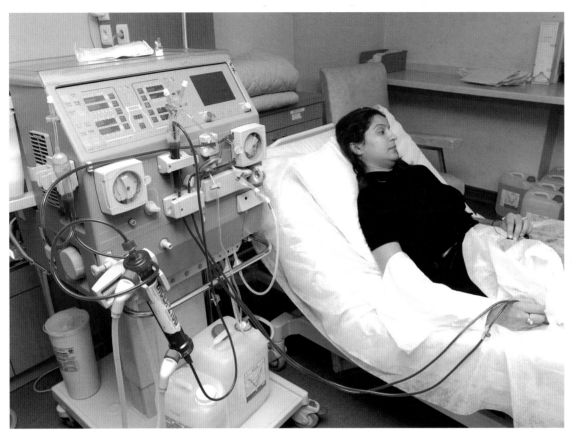

Dialysis is the process of removing blood from a patient whose kidney functioning is faulty, purifying the blood and returning it to the patient's bloodstream. Patients are usually connected to the haemodialysis machine for 3–4 hours, three times a week. The amount of time spent in hospital or connected to a machine can reduce the patient's independence and quality of life. An alternative for patients with kidney failure is a kidney transplant – this type of transplant can be done from living donors as a person only needs one functioning kidney to survive.

DIFFICULT DECISIONS FOR HANIF

Hanif Mohammed has suffered from kidney problems since he was a child, but these got worse in adult life. For the past five years, he has been on kidney dialysis which has made life difficult for the British Gas employee. As a devout Muslim, Hanif asked his religious leader, the local imam, whether a kidney transplant would be permitted. The imam said, according to his interpretation of the scriptures, Muslims could only accept an organ transplant from a living donor.

The problem arose one evening when Hanif's wife took a call from the hospital to say that they had found a suitable donor kidney for him. At first, Hanif did not know what to do because he respected the imam he had known for a long time. However, Islam does allow Muslims to ask the opinions of other imams and that was what Hanif did. As a result of talking to others and researching what other Muslim scholars had said, Hanif decided to go ahead and have the transplant.

He has recovered very well and gone on to become a black belt in several martial arts.

30 May 2008

Check you have learnt:

- two reasons why some Muslims do not permit transplant surgery
- two reasons why some Muslims will permit transplant surgery.

TRY YOUR SKILL AT THIS

The (d) question:

'Life matters most.'

In your answer you should refer to at least one religion

(i) Do you agree? Give reasons for your opinion. (3)

(ii) Give reasons why some people may disagree with you. (3)

Activity 3

What sort of reasons are the different imams likely to have given when Hanif consulted them about having a kidney transplant?

SKILLS COACHING 6

END OF CHAPTER 2 CHECK

Check the (a) question

In this chapter about *Environmental and medical issues* you learnt these **KEYWORDS**:

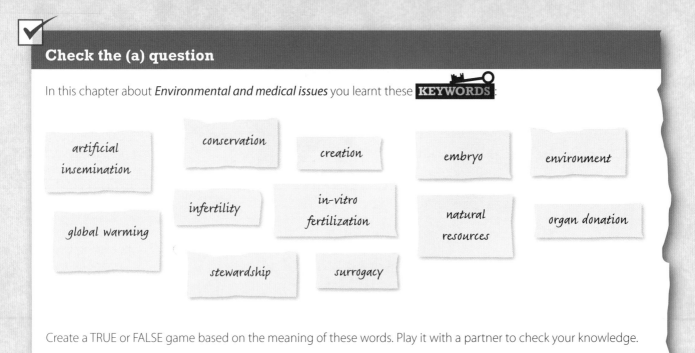

artificial insemination

conservation

creation

embryo

environment

infertility

in-vitro fertilization

natural resources

organ donation

global warming

stewardship

surrogacy

Create a TRUE or FALSE game based on the meaning of these words. Play it with a partner to check your knowledge.

Check the (c) question

Make sure that you understand:

- the major threats to the planet such as global warming, pollution and scarcity of natural resources
- Christian and Muslim teachings about stewardship
- different types of fertility treatment and the way Christians and Muslims respond to them
- transplant surgery and the different ways Christians and Muslims respond to it.

Check the (b) and (d) questions

Check you know different people's responses to the issues above for the (b) and (d) questions.

Remind yourself of the two or three reasons the other side gives to argue against you.

Obviously, your responses to the issues above are the most important ones. Rehearse two or three reasons you would give to support your viewpoint on each issue.

Finally, the vitally important thing, what religious viewpoint are you going to use for each issue?

Here is a typical example of how questions about *Environmental and medical issues* might be presented on the exam paper. Choose one of these questions to work through in exam conditions in order to check your progress.

SECTION 2 – ENVIRONMENTAL AND MEDICAL ISSUES
You must answer ONE question from this section.

EITHER

3 (a) What is meant by **artificial insemination**? (2)

   (b) Do you agree with transplant surgery?
     Give **two** reasons for your point of view. (4)

   (c) Choose **one** religion other than Christianity and explain why some
     of its followers agree with fertility treatment and some do not. (8)

   (d) 'Environmental issues are on such a large scale, individuals can do
     nothing about them.'
     In your answer you should refer to at least one religion.
     (i) Do you agree? Give reasons for your opinion. (3)
     (ii) Give reasons why some people may disagree with you. (3)
                 (Total for Question 3 = 20 marks)

OR

4 (a) What is **stewardship**? (2)

   (b) 'Nobody has the right to refuse their organs for transplant surgery
     after death.'
     Do you agree? Give **two** reasons for your point of view. (4)

   (c) Explain why religious people have a duty to care for the environment. (8)

   (d) 'Fertility treatment is every woman's right.'
     In your answer you should refer to at least one religion.
     (i) Do you agree? Give reasons for your opinion. (3)
     (ii) Give reasons why some people may disagree with you. (3)
                 (Total for Question 4 = 20 marks)

✓ If this had been the real exam, how well would you have done? Use the marking grid to check your progress. Answers to (a) appear on page 39, the grid for (b) is on page 31, the grid for (c) is on page 30 and the grid for (d) is on page 31.

CHAPTER 3

Peace and conflict

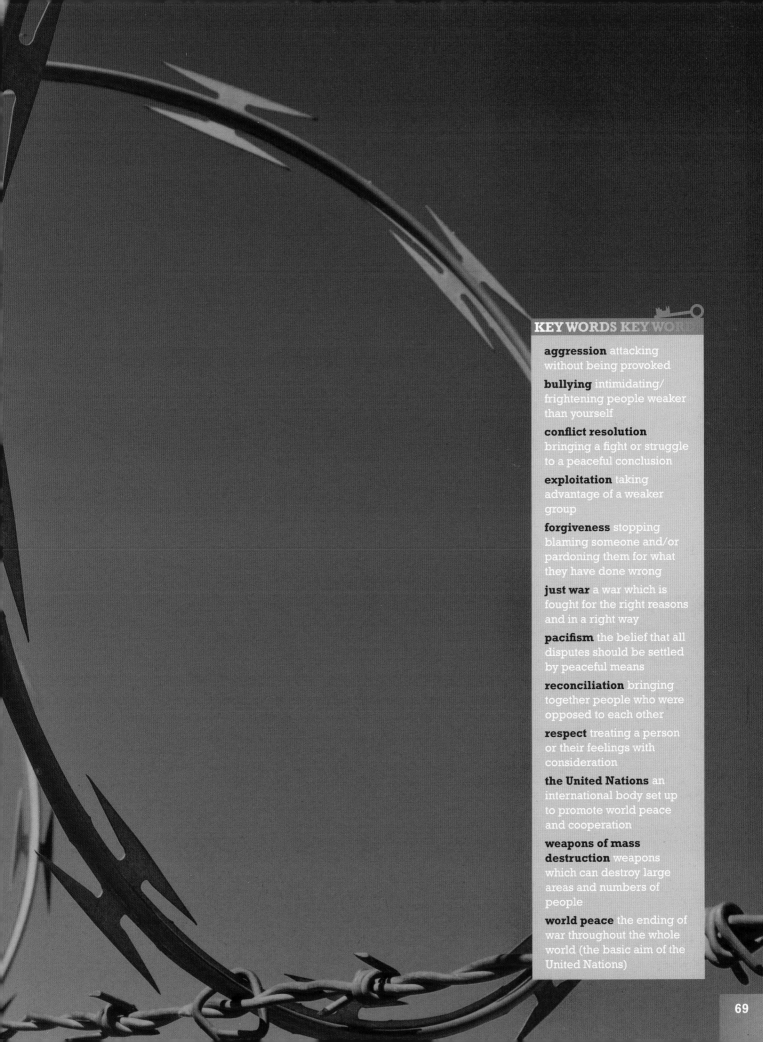

aggression attacking without being provoked

bullying intimidating/frightening people weaker than yourself

conflict resolution bringing a fight or struggle to a peaceful conclusion

exploitation taking advantage of a weaker group

forgiveness stopping blaming someone and/or pardoning them for what they have done wrong

just war a war which is fought for the right reasons and in a right way

pacifism the belief that all disputes should be settled by peaceful means

reconciliation bringing together people who were opposed to each other

respect treating a person or their feelings with consideration

the United Nations an international body set up to promote world peace and cooperation

weapons of mass destruction weapons which can destroy large areas and numbers of people

world peace the ending of war throughout the whole world (the basic aim of the United Nations)

The work of the United Nations

In this topic you will examine how the United Nations works for world peace and look at an example of its work.

The United Nations (UN) was set up after World War II to work for **world peace** and to try to prevent another global conflict ever happening. At present, 192 countries are members of the UN.

The UN has three basic aims:

1. To maintain international peace and security.
2. To develop friendly relations among countries.
3. To help countries develop economically and socially.

The UN defines the culture of peace as 'all the values, attitudes and forms of behaviour that reflect **respect** for life, for human dignity and for all human rights, the rejection of violence in all its forms and commitment to the principles of freedom, justice, solidarity and understanding between people.' In 1946, after the atrocities committed during World War II, the UN set up a Universal Declaration of Human Rights that remains the standard of welfare everyone is measured against. Work to prevent human rights abuses remains an important part of the UN's work.

The UN works towards world peace in two ways:

- By trying to resolve conflicts that have broken out. This is through peace negotiations and, once a truce has been agreed, supplying a neutral force to ensure that both sides are keeping the peace.

- By trying to prevent conflicts happening in the first place. To do this the UN has teams of skilled negotiators who try to get both sides around the table to talk through their problems and resolve them without going to war. The UN also works at tackling the sort of problems that can cause conflict, such as social and economic inequalities between countries.

These UN soldiers are part of a multi-national force, which means that neither of the warring sides can accuse the peacekeepers of being biased. UN peacekeepers are easily distinguished by their blue berets or head covering.

The UN peacekeepers

One way in which the UN promotes peace is to send a peacekeeping force into a troubled area. The UN does not have its own army, but the countries who belong to the UN voluntarily supply troops for peacekeeping duties. When the UN was first set up, the idea was that the peacekeepers would be a 'truly international peace and police force' whose job was to be present to observe things like a ceasefire but not to engage in any action.

The role of UN peacekeepers has been forced to change after atrocities like the genocide in Rwanda in 1994 and the massacre in Srebrenica the following year. Both occurred as UN forces stood by, powerless to intervene. Now, in certain situations, UN peacekeepers are instructed to enforce peace and even to intervene in disputes with force.

The UN has its headquarters on international territory in New York.

Working to remove the causes of conflict

As you will see on pages 74–75, wars break out for lots of reasons, but there are often common causes behind them. The UN has agencies that work to combat some of these problems.

- World Health Organization (WHO)
- United Nations Children's Fund (UNICEF)
- United Nations Development Programme (UNDP)
- United Nations High Commissioner for Refugees (UNHCR)
- United Nations High Commissioner for Human Rights (UNHCHR)
- United Nations Educational, Scientific and Cultural Organization (UNESCO)

CASE STUDY

The island of Cyprus has had a long troubled history with countries like Britain, Greece and Turkey all claiming ownership of it at different times. With UN help, in 1960 the island gained its independence from Britain, but later disputes arose between Turkish people in the north and Greeks in the south. Peace could only be kept between the two sides by a UN buffer zone in the middle, controlled by a peacekeeping force.

In the background, the UN continued talking to both sides to try and bring about a lasting peace and, in September 2008, the UN succeeded in getting leaders from both sides to sit down and talk about unification.

As you will see on pages 74–75

Activity 1

For discussion: 'Peacekeepers should not be allowed to fight. That doesn't make sense.' Do you agree?

Activity 2

a) Find out the name of the present Secretary-General, the leading figure of the UN.

b) Find out what sort of cases are heard at the International Court of Justice in the Hague.

c) Choose **one** of the UN agencies listed here and find out what it does. Give a presentation to the class explaining how that is linked to world peace.

✓ **Check you have learnt:**
- the aims of the UN
- how the UN works to stop conflicts starting
- how the UN works to resolve conflicts.

TRY YOUR SKILL AT THIS

The (c) question:
Describe how the UN works to promote world peace. (8)

In this topic you will study the work of two religious organizations and examine how they try to promote world peace.

The Quakers

Although there are many Christians who support peace and some who are pacifists, Quakers are the only Christian group who are totally committed to **pacifism** and non-violence.

As they explain:

"…Our conviction [is] that love is at the heart of existence and all human beings are equal in the eyes of God, and that we must live in a way that reflects this. It has led Quakers to refuse military service, and to become involved in a wide range of peace activities from practical work in areas affected by violent conflict to the development of alternatives to violence at all levels from personal to international."

At an international level, Quakers work with the UN in Geneva and New York to bring **reconciliation** between warring states. Because Quakers have no political connections, countries are often prepared to trust them with peace negotiations.

Activity 1

Describe how Quakers try to promote world peace.

Quakers believe that one way to achieve global peace and security is to rid the world of nuclear weapons. They campaign for international nuclear disarmament, both in the media and through public demonstrations.

In addition to quietly negotiating behind the scenes in Geneva, Quakers conduct a very public campaign for international disarmament. They believe this holds the key to world peace and security. They work in three ways:

- Campaigning for nuclear disarmament and the abolition of nuclear weapons in the UK and worldwide.
- Working to tackle the root causes of conflict.
- Holding meetings with UK government officials to promote a peace-building approach to foreign policy.

A united Christian approach to peace

The logo of EAPPI, a Christian group of peace workers, is clever. Notice the way the dove's feet also look like barbed wire. Ecumenical means these are Christians who come from many different traditions like Roman Catholics, Baptists, Quakers and Anglicans. What unites them is a belief in working for world peace.

The Ecumenical Accompaniment Programme in Palestine and Israel (EAPPI) was formed in 2002 to work for peace in the troubled region of Israel and Palestine (see page 74). EAPPI is made up of Christians from different Churches who are united in their resolve to promote world peace.

An accompanier is a Christian who volunteers to spend three months living with people on one side of the disputed territory. Because EAPPI supplies accompaniers to live and work on both sides of the disputed territories, they have international trust.

The accompanier is an unarmed neutral observer who provides protection by their presence. Being present can often prevent innocent civilians suffering harassment or human rights abuse. Any breaches of human rights or international and humanitarian laws that do occur are reported to the governments of Israel, Palestine, Britain and to the UN. An EAPPI also supports the work of peace activists in the communities they are living in.

This is how Paul Mukerji, an EAPPI, describes his role:

> We make a difference in small but important ways – helping individuals who had problems with permits, listening to people's stories and frustrations, showing the soldiers that the international community is there to monitor them and report on their actions and behaviour.

Activity 2

Write an advert and brief job description for an Ecumenical Accompanier that could be placed in a church magazine. Make it clear why this sort of work is important to a Christian.

Check you have learnt:

- the names of two religious organizations that are working towards world peace
- what the organizations are doing to promote world peace
- why some Christians believe this work is important.

Activity 3

What do you think Ann Wright could do to defuse the trouble that is unfolding in the photograph?

Ann Wright is an EAPPI. Here, she is standing as an observer at one of the checkpoints as two lecturers try to go to work at Nablus University. Although they have the correct ID and permits, two of them are being refused entry.

TRY YOUR SKILL AT THIS

The (d) question:

'Religious organizations should not get involved in politics.'

In your answer you should refer to at least one religion.

(i) Do you agree? Give reasons for your opinion. (3)

(ii) Give reasons why some people may disagree with you. (3)

In this topic you will consider some of the reasons why wars occur and look at some current conflicts.

What is a war?

Sadly, conflicts between humans have been going on since prehistoric times, but they have grown ever larger and kill a greater percentage of innocent civilians. Disputes between individuals aren't classed as wars, and usually small-scale conflicts within communities don't rank as wars. However, when disputes between whole communities, nationally or internationally, lead to conflict, then that is classed as a war.

What causes war?

People go to war over many things and the origins of some wars go back a long time and relate to issues that have never been properly resolved. The war in former Yugoslavia, in the late twentieth century, had its origins in a treaty at the end of World War I. The treaty carved up the Balkans in ways that took no account of the ethnic groups who lived there. Simmering resentment finally erupted into war in the 1990s.

The Arab-Israeli War (see Case study 1 below) also has its origins in a long-term dispute.

Some of the causes of conflict are:

- **Religious reasons** – religious differences have been the cause of many wars in history. From the medieval Crusades, when Christians tried to force people to convert to Christianity, through to Roman Catholics and Protestants fighting each other in Northern Ireland in the twentieth century.
- **Economic reasons** – when one country grabs land or wealth from another by force. In the past, the wealth may have been gold and silver; today, it is likely to be oil or mineral resources. This can lead to the **exploitation** of a small country by a more powerful one.
- **Social reasons** – this may happen when one community wants to force another group to behave in the same way as they do, or attacks them because of their ethnic differences.
- **Moral reasons** – this might be because one community feels obliged to attack another to restore the inhabitants' human rights.

KEY WORDS KEY WORDS

exploitation taking advantage of a weaker group

weapons of mass destruction weapons which can destroy large areas and numbers of people

aggression attacking without being provoked

Activity 1

a) In groups, each take a different daily newspaper and go through it to see if there are any references to wars going on around the world at the present time.

b) Discover who is involved in the conflict and what the reasons are.

c) Share your findings with the class.

CASE STUDY 1

The Arab-Israeli conflict

The area that is known as modern-day Israel has been disputed territory for more than 2000 years. The Jews believe Israel is the land God promised them in the Bible but, by the time of Jesus, the country was occupied by the Romans. Later, it was conquered by the Turks and ruled by them for 400 years as Palestine. In 1948, following World War II, the UN set up a new state of Israel as a homeland for the Jews. A separate area of the country, named Palestine, was partitioned off and given to the Arabs who had previously occupied the whole state. Arguments about who has rights to the land and access to religious sites – holy to Jews, Muslims and Christians – have raged ever since. Skirmishes have erupted into brief wars and terrorist attacks have poisoned relations between both sides.

In December 2008 and January 2009, the Palestinian territory of Gaza endured the worst bombing raid in its history when Israeli armed forces attacked them to stop rockets being launched at their lands.

CASE STUDY 2

The Iraq War

The conflict that began in Iraq in 2003 shows how complex the causes of war can be. American and British forces attacked Iraq because they believed Iraq had **weapons of mass destruction** that could be used to threaten the West. It later transpired that Iraq did not possess these weapons. US and UK leaders also said that the intention of the Iraq War was to free the country from the dictator Saddam Hussein, who abused the Iraqi people's human rights. Critics of the war said that the real reason for the invasion was economic because the USA wanted access to Iraq's huge oil fields. Some people say that the USA and UK showed **aggression** by attacking a country that had not threatened them. The leaders argued that the war was justified to prevent an attack.

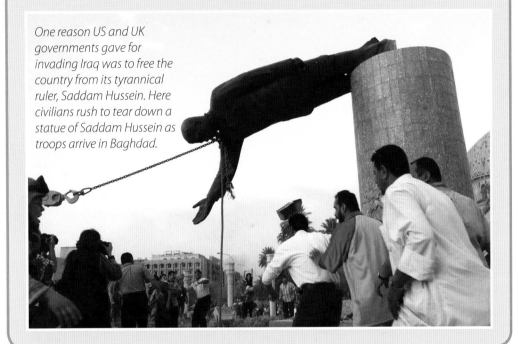

One reason US and UK governments gave for invading Iraq was to free the country from its tyrannical ruler, Saddam Hussein. Here civilians rush to tear down a statue of Saddam Hussein as troops arrive in Baghdad.

Activity 2

For discussion: Is it justified to invade a country:

- that has not threatened you?
- to free its inhabitants?
- to stop it attacking you in the future?
- because you think its leaders are evil?

✓ Check you have learnt:

- three causes of war
- details of one recent conflict.

TRY YOUR SKILL AT THIS

The (c) question:

Explain why wars can occur in the twenty-first century. (8)

SKILLS COACHING 7

DO YOU KNOW?

Improve your skill with the (a) question

Check you know the meaning of the **KEYWORDS** that have already appeared in this chapter. In fact, most of the words for this chapter have already appeared:

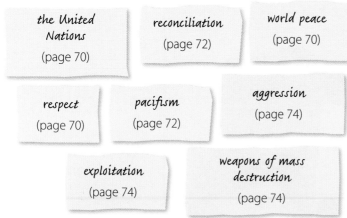

the United Nations
(page 70)

reconciliation
(page 72)

world peace
(page 70)

respect
(page 70)

pacifism
(page 72)

aggression
(page 74)

exploitation
(page 74)

weapons of mass destruction
(page 74)

✳ TRY THIS ✳

Write every keyword and its meaning down on separate cards. Cut out the keyword and its meaning separately. With a partner, lay all the cards with the keywords face upwards on the desk. Lay all the meanings face down in a pile. Take it in turns to draw a card with a meaning from the pile.

You score a point if you can place the meaning on top of the correct keyword. Incorrect meanings go back into the pack, which is then shuffled, to be drawn again.

Improve your skill with the (c) question

The (c) questions so far in this chapter are likely to concentrate on the reasons why wars occur and what different organizations are doing to promote peace. Remember that questions about the causes of war will be asking you to show that you not only understand some of the causes, but that you can refer to some examples of recent conflicts.

In addition to the *Explain why* questions you studied in Skills coaching 5 (page 58), you might also be asked to *Explain how* something has occurred:

> Explain **how** and **why** some organizations work towards world peace.　　　　(8)

Here is Mai Li's attempt to answer this:

> Some organizations like the United Nations (UN) think it is a good thing for countries around the world to get on with each other. This is because it is better for everybody. People don't get injured or have their houses destroyed.
>
> What the UN does is to send in soldiers with blue berets to keep the peace and they try to get countries talking.

You are the examiner. Look to see where Mai Li has explained **how** and where she has explained **why**. Use the grid to mark her answer and then write a brief note saying what she could have done to get a higher grade.

Level 1	• One brief reason. • Not explaining but describing the issue.	1–2 marks
Level 2	• Two brief reasons. • One expanded reason.	3–4 marks
Level 3	• Three brief reasons. • One fully-developed reason. • Two reasons with one expanded.	5–6 marks
Level 4	• Four brief reasons. • Two expanded reasons. • Three reasons with one expanded.	7–8 marks

WHAT DO YOU THINK?

Improve your skill with the (b) question

The (b) question will be asking for you to state your opinions loud and clear! Here are a few statements for you to voice an opinion on:

'World peace is impossible; it's a waste of time trying.'
'Only the weak are pacifists.'
'Wars are always caused by religion.'
Do you agree? Give **two** reasons for your point of view. (4)

For each of these statements, write **two** reasons you would respond with.

Here is Sonny's answer to the second statement, along with the examiner's marking. See if you can understand why the examiner decided to award the marks.

I don't think pacifists are weak because you have got to be pretty brave to refuse to fight. ✓ (1 mark for a brief reason) But if you chose to do medical work instead of killing people, that shows courage. ✓ (1 mark) Some of them have to go on to the battlefield and collect the injured. ✓ (1 mark for expanded reason) It takes a lot of courage to take a stand against war when the media are talking it up. ✓ (1 mark for expanded reason)

Improve your skill with the (d) question

The (d) question is looking for two contrasting arguments, so try these quotations:

'War provides a quicker solution than peace talks.'
'Weapons of mass destruction can never be justified.'
'Religious people only talk about peace but they don't do much.'
'Everybody has a duty to fight for their country.'

The question goes on to ask:

In your answer you should refer to at least one religion.
(i) Do you agree? Give reasons for your opinion. (3)
(ii) Give reasons why some people may disagree with you. (3)

This was how Steve answered the second quotation above:

(i) I agree that weapons of mass destruction (WMD) are terrible because they kill anybody even the innocent. It's a fact that more civilians get killed in wars than soldiers. I think chemical weapons are bad too. They poison the ground and that sort of thing, so people can't even lead a normal life when the conflict ends.

(ii) But some people say that because WMDs are so terrible, nobody dares to use them. This keeps the peace.

Use the grid to award marks to parts (i) and (ii) of Steve's answer. Then write a couple of sentences explaining why Steve was given that grade.

Level 1	● One brief reason.	1 mark
Level 2	● Two brief reasons. ● One expanded reason.	2 marks
Level 3	● Three brief reasons. ● Two expanded reasons. ● One fully-developed reason.	3 marks

3.4

A just war

In this topic you will study the nature and importance of the theory of a just war.

KEY WORDS KEY WOR

just war a war which is fought for the right reasons and in a right way

What does a just war mean?

Some people believe that, no matter how desirable peace is, there may be very good reasons why it is necessary to go to war in some situations. Refusing to fight could allow evil to win.

Ever since medieval times, philosophers have worked on drawing up rules to define when it is right to go to war and the fairest way to conduct a war so that it results in the minimum of destruction and suffering. These are considered to be the rules for a **just war**.

The Christian philosopher and monk, Thomas Aquinas, worked on some of the earliest rules. Although he lived in the fourth century CE, his theory of a just war remains the basis of the rules used by the West today.

The theory of a just war

1. **The war must be for a just cause.** This includes resisting aggression, or for self-defence or fighting to remove an injustice.

2. **A war must be declared by a lawful authority.** A war can only be declared by a government, a ruler or the UN, but never by a private citizen.

3. **A war must only be fought to bring about good.** This means that a war can be fought to restore peace, or to prevent further suffering or any other form of evil. Once that end has been achieved, fighting must stop.

4. **War must be a last resort.** All other peaceful ways of resolving the problem, such as negotiations, must be tried first.

5. **There must be a reasonable chance of success.** This means that no country is to go to war when they stand no chance of winning. This is to prevent lives being lost unnecessarily.

6. **Only necessary force must be used to achieve the aim.** This means that it would be totally unjustified to use nuclear weapons against a small country over something like a boundary dispute. The clause is intended to prevent one country taking the opportunity of a war to totally annihilate the other.

7. **Only legitimate targets should be attacked.** These would be military installations and other soldiers. Hospitals, homes and civilians are not to be attacked.

Activity 1

Read the rules of a just war. Give all the reasons why a terrorist bomb attack at a tube station is unjust.

Activity 2

The USA and the UK attacked Iraq in 2003 without waiting for official permission from the UN. Why would some people say that the Iraq War was not a just war?

The widespread destruction caused by a nuclear bomb, and the fact that the land is unusable for many years afterwards, caused some people to question whether weapons of mass destruction can ever be justified.

Activity 3

a) In 1963, Pope John XXIII said, 'It is impossible to conceive of a just war in a nuclear age.' Do you agree?

b) Read the criteria of a just war. Are there any rules that would be broken if weapons of mass destruction were used?

Check you have learnt:

- what is meant by a just war
- at least three points that relate to a just war
- reasons why it is important to have rules about war.

TRY YOUR SKILL AT THIS

The (b) question:
'War can never be justified.' Do you agree? Give **two** reasons for your point of view. (4)

Why does the just war theory matter?

Having rules about when it is right to go to war and the way in which a war is to be fought is important in a civilized society. It forces a country to stop and weigh up what it is about to do before engaging in a war. This could make a peaceful outcome to the dispute more likely. The rules of engagement ensure that a war is fought with the minimum of destruction and suffering.

What is the Christian attitude to war?

In this topic you will examine the differences among Christians in their attitudes to war and the reasons for them.

The majority of Christians accept that war can be a necessary evil. Although they would prefer everyone to live in peace, they understand that sometimes fighting is the only way to overcome evil. Scenes like those when the death camp at Auschwitz was liberated convince many Christians that World War II was justified to put an end to the atrocities suffered by Jews and others at the hands of the Nazi regime.

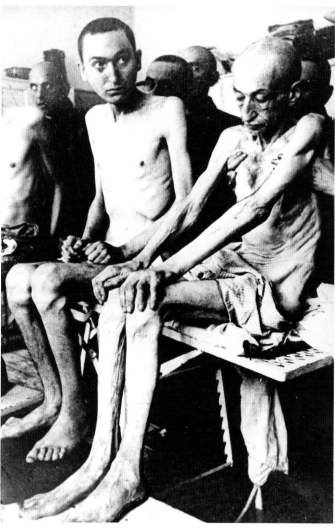

Scenes like this, the liberation of people in the death camp at Auschwitz at the end of World War II, convince most Christians that sometimes war is the best solution.

What was Jesus' attitude to war?

Jesus lived in a country that was under military occupation, but he never condemned the soldiers. Indeed, in Luke 7:1–10 Jesus praised the Roman soldier for his faith. On another occasion when Jesus was asked whether it was correct to pay taxes to the Romans, he said, 'Give to Caesar what is Caesar's.' Christians interpret this to mean that they should obey the state orders, and this includes fighting in a just war (see pages 78–79) to overcome evil and reinstate good.

St Paul also reinforced the idea of a just war when he said:

> *Everyone must obey the state authorities, because no authority exists without God's permission, and the existing authorities have been put there by God.*
>
> **(Romans 13:1)**

Although many Christians accept that war may be justified, the Churches have been outspoken in their concern about many aspects of modern warfare. This is because, despite the alleged surgical precision of many weapons, most casualties of war are civilians.

The Roman Catholic Church

CAFOD says:

> "War and conflict have a direct impact on development. In times of war crops are destroyed, or people may be forced to leave their homes before they can plant or harvest crops. Millions of people flee areas where there is fighting to look for safety.
> Anti-personnel landmines make land unusable. Roads and bridges are destroyed, schools and health clinics closed."

Pope Benedict XVI said:

> I'd say that we cannot ignore, in the great Christian tradition and in a world marked by sin, any evil aggression that threatens to destroy not only many values, many people, but the image of humanity itself.
>
> In this case, defending oneself and others is a duty. Let's say for example that a father who sees his family attacked is duty-bound to defend them in every way possible – even if that means using proportional violence [that is, the same amount of violence as the attacker is using].

Christian pacifists

Some Christians are pacifists, which means they believe war is never justified. They point out that Jesus preached the message of love and peace. Because Jesus is often called the Prince of Peace, some Christians believe they should work for **conflict resolution** through peaceful means rather than go to war.

Jesus said:

> Do not take revenge on someone who wrongs you. If anyone slaps you on the right cheek, let him slap your left cheek too. **(Matthew 5:39)**

Within all Christian denominations there are some people who are against war, but the Quakers are the only Christian group who are totally pacifist. They think that violence is always destructive and can never achieve any lasting peace.

The Quakers say:

> Quakers in Britain have always opposed the use of violence in any form, for any end. Instead we work to build the conditions of peace that "take away the occasion of all wars".
>
> Quakers believe that conflict can be a positive force for change, if handled creatively, but it is the use of violence, or the threat of violence, as a means of dealing with conflict, that is problematic … The use of violence to bring about change may create temporary good, but also increases the chance of violence becoming a permanent way of resolving conflict.

Activity 1

CAFOD is the Catholic Agency for Overseas Development. Why would they be especially concerned about war?

Activity 2

Draw two columns on your page. Using the information on these pages, list the reasons in one column why some Christians agree war may be necessary and, in the other column, why some Christians are pacifists.

Activity 3

What reasons does the Pope give for permitting war?

Some Quakers joined peace activists in a year-long blockade of the Faslane nuclear weapons base in Scotland as a protest against Britain's Trident nuclear weapons system.

 Check you have learnt:

- what is meant by pacifist
- why some Christians believe war may be right
- why some Christians are pacifists.

Activity 4

a) What reason do some Christians give for being pacifists?

b) What is your view of pacifism?

TRY YOUR SKILL AT THIS

The (c) question:

Explain why some Christians would say that war may be acceptable. (8)

Useful specialist terms

jihad means to strive

greater jihad is the struggle within a person to resist temptation and do good rather than evil

lesser jihad is a military struggle to defend Islam

Although Islam is a religion of peace, Muslims do not believe in pacifism. The Qur'an teaches that sometimes war is necessary to conquer evil but, once evil has been defeated, fighting must stop and peace be restored.

Jihad

A Muslim's life is directed towards pleasing Allah, and this involves getting rid of evil and establishing a peaceful society on earth. The struggle against evil is called jihad, but the Qur'an teaches Muslims that the struggle against evil must first start within themselves.

The greater jihad is the personal battle that everyone has with themselves, whether to do what is right or succumb to temptation and do what we know is wrong.

Muslims also understand that, on occasions, it may be necessary to fight against evil in the world. Taking military action in order to bring about a just society is called the lesser jihad and Muslims should go to war if that is necessary. They must also fight to preserve Islam if the religion comes under attack.

A holy war

Muslims also have rules about how war (the lesser jihad) should be conducted. These rules are similar to those for a just war, but the conflict is more usually referred to as a holy war.

Many Muslims thought that the invasion of Iraq by the USA and the UK was unjust. They joined non-Muslims in staging peaceful protests in London and elsewhere around the world.

The theory of a holy war

- **War must be a last resort**, which means that every effort should be made to solve the dispute by non-violent means.

- **A war can only be started and controlled by a religious leader** but Islam teaches Muslims that they must not be the first to declare war.

- **War must have a just cause**, which might be self-defence to prevent people suffering injustice or to protect the religion from attack.

- **The aim of a war must be to bring about good**. Muslims are taught that it is wrong to fight as an act of aggression or to conquer another country. The aim has to be to bring about a just society.

- **Killing must not be indiscriminate, innocent civilians should not suffer** – these particularly include women, children and the elderly.

- **Once the aim has been achieved, fighting must stop, mercy be shown and peace restored.**

In addition to these rules, there are many others about the conduct of a holy war, such as treating wounded enemies in exactly the same way as Muslims treat their own wounded. The women and children of the enemy side must not be harmed; neither should any trees, crops or animals. Prophet Muhammad was himself involved in fighting wars to establish peace, and Muslims look to his teachings and his example when deciding the right conduct of war.

Guidance from the Qur'an

> *If they incline to peace, make peace with them, and put your trust in God. It is surely He who hears all and knows all.* (Qur'an 8:61)

> *Paradise is for those who curb their anger and forgive their fellow men.* (Qur'an 3:134)

> *Good deeds and evil deeds are not equal. Requite evil with good, and he who is your enemy will become your dearest friend.* (Qur'an 41:34)

> *Fight for the sake of God those that fight against you. But do not attack them first.* (Qur'an 2:190)

> *There should be no compulsion in religion.* (Qur'an 2:256)

The obligation to fight

The Qur'an and the teachings of Muhammad tell Muslims that if all the criteria of a holy war are fulfilled, it is their religious duty to go to war. Any Muslim killed whilst fighting a holy war is a martyr and will go directly to paradise.

Muslims must fight if their religion is being threatened.

Activity 1

List the points these quotations from the Qur'an teach Muslims about the conduct of a holy war.

Activity 2

a) Read the conditions of a holy war. Why do some Muslims believe that the use of nuclear weapons can never be justified?

b) Do you think it is acceptable to use weapons of mass destruction in warfare? (This includes biological as well as nuclear weapons.)

Activity 3

Explain why some Muslims might say that tabloid newspapers misrepresent the concept of jihad.

✓ Check you have learnt:

- the meaning of jihad, the lesser and the greater jihad
- four points necessary for a holy war
- the Muslim attitude to peace.

TRY YOUR SKILL AT THIS

The (c) question:

Choose **one** *religion other than Christianity* and explain why its followers would say that terrorism is not acceptable. (8)

What is the Christian attitude towards bullying?

In this topic you will study what is meant by bullying, Christian attitudes towards bullying and the reasons for these attitudes.

What is bullying?

bullying intimidating/ frightening people weaker than yourself

This might seem a pointless question because everybody knows what bullying is because, sadly, most people experience it at one time or another. The term **bullying** is used to cover all forms of intimidation, both physical and mental. People often think that bullying is something that only happens to children in school, but it happens to all ages and in all places. People at work sometimes find themselves intimidated by managers or others in authority. Elderly people in care homes sometimes experience bullying at the hands of those who should be looking after them. What these situations have in common is that one person feels superior and makes someone else suffer. It's wrong and we all know that!

St Paul told Christians:

> *"Love your neighbour as you love yourself." If you love someone, you will never do them wrong; to love, then, is to obey the whole Law.* (Romans 13:9–10)

Bullying is a form of human rights abuse that affects all age groups.

What is the Christian attitude to bullying?

Christians are against all forms of bullying because it makes people suffer. Christians believe that everybody was created by God and the Bible says they were made in the image of God. This means that treating someone badly is abusing God's creation. The Bible also teaches that everybody is equal in the eyes of God, so no one has the right to treat anyone as inferior by bullying them.

Christians are totally against any form of discrimination because it goes against everything Jesus taught his followers. The Golden Rule says, 'Treat others as you would like to be treated yourself.' A Christian who follows Jesus' teachings would interpret that to mean all forms of bullying are unacceptable.

The Gospels contain many other teachings about treating people as equals and showing them respect as human beings. This all leads a Christian to understand that bullying can never be right.

Jesus preached a message of love that leads Christians to work for the prevention of suffering. Some Christians choose to support the work of a charity like The Children's Society, which assists victims of bullying.

The Children's Society was set up by a Christian to help children living on the streets in Victorian times. Its work has changed with the times and, today, it helps children who face danger, discrimination or disadvantage in their daily lives. Anti-bullying is a key area the society has been working on. In the Rochdale area, it has trained a team of adults to work in schools to prevent bullying and to help young people who are suffering bullying.

Activity 1

Design an A5 leaflet that could be distributed at a church youth club. On one side, it should urge young people to report any instances of bullying. On the other side, it should explain why Christians believe that bullying is wrong.

Activity 2

a) Give **three** different situations where bullying might occur.

b) Give **four** reasons why bullying is wrong.

c) Give **two** examples of the long-term harm bullying might cause a person.

 Check you have learnt:

- what is meant by bullying
- three reasons why Christians know bullying is wrong
- two ways in which Christians might work to stop bullying.

TRY YOUR SKILL AT THIS

The (d) question:

'If everybody followed religious teachings, it would put an end to bullying.'

In your answer you should refer to at least one religion.

(i) Do you agree? Give reasons for your opinion. (3)

(ii) Give reasons why some people may disagree with you. (3)

In this topic you will study Muslim attitudes towards bullying and the reasons for these attitudes.

Bullying is evil

Islam totally condemns all forms of bullying. Islam is a religion of peace and bullying goes against everything the religion stands for. There are many teachings that lead Muslims to understand this.

- The Qur'an teaches Muslims that Allah created every human being and everyone is equal in the eyes of Allah. This means that everybody should be shown respect as part of Allah's creation. Therefore, it would be completely wrong to intimidate another person in any way.
- Bullying is a form of injustice and Islam teaches that all forms of injustice are wrong. Muslims are taught that it is their duty to fight injustice in the world, not to cause it by bullying.
- Muslims are taught to show compassion to the weak, which might lead a Muslim to help someone who is the victim of bullying.
- Islam teaches Muslims that they are all brothers in the *ummah*, so it would be wrong to bully a fellow Muslim.
- There are specific religious teachings telling a Muslim how they should treat different relatives like husbands and wives, children and the elderly. All direct Muslims to show respect and compassion towards them, not aggression.

> *Allah will not show mercy to the one who does not show mercy to others.*
> **(Hadith)**

The judgement of Allah

Muslims believe that everything a person does in their life is known to Allah. After death, everyone will go before Allah to be judged on the way they behaved in their life. Those who have done wrong will be punished. Bullying is a serious sin. Those who show compassion to others by helping the victims of bullying will be rewarded by Allah.

Useful specialist terms

ummah the brotherhood of all Muslims, whether male or female

Activity 1

Make a poster with '**Islam condemns bullies**' written in the centre. Display the reasons for this around the outside.

Cyber bullying is a growing problem. Islam totally condemns all forms of bullying.

Cyber bullying

Although bullying has been around as long as there have been people on earth, with the introduction of electronic communication bullying has taken on a more sinister form. Cyber bullying involves a person using a mobile phone or the Internet to intimidate someone. This is a particularly nasty and cowardly form of bullying that is totally condemned by Muslims and everybody else.

This charity works with schools and young people to keep them safe from bullying. They have set up CyberMentors, the social networking site run by young people for young people who help and support their peers in an online virtual community. CyberMentors are fully trained and act as mentors and guides to young people they meet online when chatting, surfing and just generally having fun.

This UK charity works with young people under the age of 16. Their work is vital because research shows that bullying leads to great unhappiness and makes children six times more likely to contemplate suicide. They say that 1 in 12 children are badly bullied to the point that it affects their education, relationships and even their prospects for jobs in later life. Although this charity has no religious connections, its work is something Muslims would support.

preventing bullying, protecting children

Activity 2

a) Prepare a piece to go on your school's website explaining why bullying is wrong. You can use religious reasons from Islam, or Christianity, or non-religious reasons.

b) Create another screen that suggests **three** ways in which schools could tackle bullying.

Activity 3

For discussion: Some people say that forcing a person to follow the same religion as their parents is a form of bullying. Do you agree? Why?

Check you have learnt:
- what the Muslim attitude towards bullying is
- two reasons why Muslims are against bullying
- why bullying is unjust.

TRY YOUR SKILL AT THIS
The (c) question:
Explain why a Muslim should never bully anyone. (8)

SKILLS COACHING 8

Improve your skill with the (a) question

Keyword meanings	Keyword	Mark
A war which is fought for the right reasons and in a right way.		
The belief that all disputes should be settled by peaceful means.		
An international body set up to promote world peace and cooperation.		
Intimidating/frightening people weaker than yourself.		
Bringing together people who were opposed to each other.		

✳ TRY THIS ✳

Copy down each of the keyword meanings. Write the correct keyword alongside. Then mark your answers according to the definitions on page 69.

Improve your skill with the (c) question

The two major topics you studied in the last section were attitudes to war and attitudes to bullying. Make sure that you understand the different attitudes Christians have towards war and can give the reasons for their views.

Islam is more straightforward on this issue because this religion permits war. But, like all groups, not all Muslims agree with the idea of war. Therefore, if you are asked to consider different attitudes towards war in this religion, you need to think about why some people disagree with it. Reasons you could give, in addition to interpretations of scriptures, are that people get hurt and wars result in widespread destruction of property and businesses. People without religious beliefs might give these reasons as well, but that doesn't make any difference, they are still valid. It's always worth remembering the reasons anybody might give, religious or otherwise, to an issue if you are struggling with an answer. Don't forget, religious people are still people!

Keep the above in mind when developing full answers to questions about war and bullying. Try **one** of these (c) questions and don't forget your QWC!

Explain why some Christians think war is acceptable. (8)

Explain why members of **one** *religion other than Christianity* would think bullying is wrong. (8)

Choose **one** *religion other than Christianity* and explain why justice is central to their attitude to war. (8)

STEP 1
Copy out the question, underlining the most important words. Is the question asking for more than one viewpoint?

STEP 2
Jot down as many points as you can think of.

STEP 3
Develop the points into full sentences and support them with reasons.

WHAT DO YOU THINK?

Improve your skill with the (d) question

War is a very controversial issue as you know and, for this reason, it could well appear as a (d) question. 'War is never the right solution.' This could form the basis of a (b) or a (d) question because it is challenging you to reply.

You could answer it from the point of view of the reasons why wars occur in the first place. This enables you to discuss whether it is better to tackle the causes of war rather than simply fight and make the situation worse.

You could also look at it from the point of view that fighting is destructive. This enables you to consider peace negotiations and the United Nations' efforts to avoid war. You might also want to discuss whether pacifism achieves anything worthwhile, or even whether it works at all.

Try out your answer to this statement as a (d) question:

> 'War is never the right solution.'
> In your answer you should refer to at least one religion.
> (i) Do you agree? Give reasons for your opinion. (3)
> (ii) Give reasons why some people may disagree with you. (3)

Imran began:

> *(i) I think you might have to go to war if your country is threatened. I wouldn't want to stand by and see my family shot for nothing.*

Complete Imran's part (i) with another reason and write part (ii) for him.

Another controversial area is whether there is such a thing as a just war. You need to ask yourself whether it is realistic to have rules about how war is conducted. Will countries obey them and do the rules of a just war stop people suffering? It is also worth asking yourself whether war should have anything to do with religious ideas at all.

Here is a (d) question:

> 'Religion should keep out of warfare.'
> In your answer you should refer to at least one religion.
> (i) Do you agree? Give reasons for your opinion. (3)
> (ii) Give reasons why some people may disagree with you. (3)

Callum wrote this:

> *I think religion is the cause of wars so they ought to get involved in ending them. If there wasn't so much religion, there wouldn't be any war. Some Christians are good at keeping the peace, so they ought to be allowed to go and talk to the other side to see if they can stop the war. But religious people are people so it's not surprising they get involved in fights. They wouldn't like it if someone forced them to follow a religion they didn't agree with.*

Look closely at Callum's answer, which is very weak and has muddled everything up. Can you find an answer to part (i)? What sort of reasons has he given? Is there any material to answer part (ii)? Has Callum included any reasons?

Here is the marking grid for parts (i) and (ii). How many marks does Callum score?

Level 1	• One brief reason.	1 mark
Level 2	• Two brief reasons. • One expanded reason.	2 marks
Level 3	• Three brief reasons. • Two expanded reasons. • One fully-developed reason.	3 marks

> In this topic you will explore what happens when there are religious conflicts in families.

Activity 1

a) What problems do you think might arise in a Christian family if a teenager dates someone from a different religion?

b) How far do you think a teenager should be dictated to by their parents over this sort of issue?

*The film **East is East** explored, with humour, religious conflicts in a family in Salford.*

Although most people want a peaceful home life, tensions do arise within families. We are all individuals, so it's not surprising we don't always see eye to eye with each other. Living within a family can offer wonderful support but, sadly, on occasion, feelings can boil over, tensions grow and conflicts can arise. Because religion involves all aspects of a person's life, any religious conflicts within a family can be difficult to resolve.

The film *East is East*, which came out several years ago, was concerned with religious conflicts in a working-class family. Tensions stemmed from the fact that the parents come from different religions; the father is a Muslim and his wife a Roman Catholic. The parents themselves cope with their religious differences fairly easily. The only area of concern between them is that Islam permits a man to have up to four wives and the Catholic wife is aware that her husband has another wife living in Pakistan.

It is the children in the family who experience the most religious conflicts. As young teenagers, they struggle to obey the religion their father requires them to follow and the modern lifestyle of their friends.

Reasons for religious conflicts in families

Here are the religious conflicts that arose in the film, but some might equally arise in any family:

- **Arranged marriage**. It is the duty of a Muslim father to assist his children in finding the correct marriage partner. This might cause a problem in a family where the children feel they have a right to choose their own partner, or even whether they marry at all.

- **Same-sex relationships**. Some religions, like Islam, believe that same-sex relationships are totally wrong. This could cause a problem, as it did in *East is East,* if one person in the family is gay.

- **Dress**. Some religions, like Islam, have rules about dressing modestly at all times. This may cause conflicts in a family where young people want to dress like their peers. No Muslim parent could allow their child to dress in a sexually provocative way because it is against the teachings of the Qur'an. Whilst many parents might object to revealing clothing, there are no Christian rules about dress.

- **Diet**. Religions like Islam and Judaism have dietary rules set out in the holy scriptures. In the film *East is East*, the teenagers enjoyed eating bacon which is permitted by their Catholic mother but forbidden by their Muslim father. There is much humour in the film as they try to get rid of the smell when they hear their father returning unexpectedly.

- **Authority**. Many religions have rules about authority within the family. In Islam, children should respect their parents and obey their father. Whilst respect is also important in Christianity, only some traditional Christian families put the father firmly at the head of the household. Many Christian families believe that the parents have equal authority within the family. Conflicts might arise in a multi-faith family.

- **Which religion to follow?** This might cause conflict in a multi-faith family where both husband and wife believe it is their religious duty to bring a child up in their own faith. A Muslim man has a duty to bring up his children as Muslims and Catholics have a duty to bring up their children as Catholics.

- **Attitudes to sexual relationships**. Young people growing up in a religious family would be brought up to believe that sexual relationships belong within marriage. This might cause conflicts with young people who want to cohabit before they marry. Issues of contraception might also be a source of conflict between couples from different religions.

- **Traditional roles**. Traditionalists in most religions believe that the woman's role is that of home-maker and the man's is to provide for his family. This might cause conflict for a couple in today's society where these roles are more flexible and single-parent families are common.

Activity 2

Write a response to each of the problem-page letters below.

> ❝ I love my parents and wouldn't want to hurt them. But I don't see why I have to go to church and give up alcohol for Lent just because they choose to. Why should I? ❞
>
> **Sam (18)**

> ❝ It is my duty to give Sophie the best possible start in life. Following the true religion that she has been brought up in is the only way. She is rebelling against it. What should I do? ❞
>
> **Worried mother (Bristol)**

Check you have learnt:

- two reasons why religious conflicts may occur in families
- four different things that might spark a religious conflict.

TRY YOUR SKILL AT THIS

The (c) question:

Explain why religion might cause conflict in some families. (8)

In this topic you will examine Christian teachings on forgiveness and reconciliation.

Forgiveness and reconciliation are at the heart of Jesus' teachings and, for this reason, both are important to Christians. Jesus not only taught forgiveness, he practised it in his own life.

As he was dying on the cross, Jesus said, 'Forgive them, Father! They don't know what they are doing.' (Luke 23:34)

KEY WORDS KEY WORDS

forgiveness stopping blaming someone and/or pardoning them for what they have done wrong

Activity 1

For discussion: Is it a sign of weakness to forgive somebody? How many times do you think it is right to forgive a person who has done wrong, but is genuine in their apology?

Activity 2

The Parable of the Lost Son in Luke 15:11–32 is an important Christian teaching about forgiveness and reconciliation.

a) What wrong was done?

b) Was any apology given?

c) How was forgiveness shown?

d) Who could not accept reconciliation?

e) The father represents God in the story. What does this teach Christians about forgiveness?

What did Jesus teach?

Through parables, Jesus taught his followers that it is vital they forgive people who harm them. Peter asked Jesus how many times he should forgive somebody who continues to hurt him; 'Seven times?' Peter suggested. But Jesus answered, 'No, not seven times … but seventy times seven' (Matthew 18:21–22), which Christians believe means an infinite number of times. Jesus' teachings about forgiveness were revolutionary and, even today, many Christians find them hard to put into practice.

> *Do not take revenge on someone who wrongs you … love your enemies and pray for those who persecute you.* **(Matthew 5:39 and 44)**

Jesus also taught his followers that forgiveness is a two-way thing:

> *Forgive us the wrongs that we have done, as we forgive the wrongs that others have done to us.* **(Matthew 6:12)**

What Jesus was also saying was that if Christians do not forgive people who hurt them, they cannot expect God to forgive them for their sins.

Forgiveness and reconciliation in action

> Some people think reconciliation is a soft option, that it means papering over the cracks. But the biblical meaning means looking facts in the face and it can be very costly; it cost God the death of his own Son.

As a Christian, Archbishop Desmond Tutu is committed to forgiveness and reconciliation as the only way forward.

After years of human rights abuse in South Africa, the country elected its first black president, Nelson Mandela, in 1994. But South Africa had a history of atrocities between blacks and whites. This was a past that couldn't be forgotten, but how could people be reconciled to it?

The way forward was the Truth and Reconciliation Commission (TRC). People were encouraged to come forward and tell the truth about crimes they had committed or atrocities they had suffered. In return for the truth, people would be granted a pardon and victims would receive help. Nobody was to be interrogated or punished; all that was required was truth.

Reconciliation meant that everyone had to accept what had happened and not seek revenge. Although people spoke of, and listened to, terrible atrocities, the truth brought opposing sides together to forgive and bring closure to the past.

The TRC was led by Archbishop Tutu who said, 'There is no future for South Africa without forgiveness. Revenge will lead to a blood-bath. Forgiving and forgetting will allow South Africa to move forward.' Despite people's doubts, this proved to be the right approach.

Activity 3

In pairs, discuss what happens if someone apologizes but it is not accepted. Does this mean forgiveness and reconciliation is a two-way process?

Check you have learnt:

- what Christians mean by forgiveness
- two of Jesus' teachings about forgiveness
- reasons why Christians think reconciliation is the best way forward.

Activity 4

Write a piece for a Christian website explaining how the TRC put Christian teachings of forgiveness and reconciliation into practice.

TRY YOUR SKILL AT THIS

The (d) question:

'Some crimes are so horrible that forgiveness would be wrong.'

In your answer, you should refer to at least one religion.

(i) Do you agree? Give reasons for your opinion. (3)

(ii) Give reasons why some people may disagree with you. (3)

In this topic you will examine Muslim teachings on forgiveness and reconciliation.

Muslims learn about the importance of forgiveness from three key areas.

1 The teachings of the Qur'an

Muslims are taught that it is important to forgive someone who has done them wrong because Allah will forgive them their sins.

> *Better and more enduring is God's reward to those who believe and put their trust in Him; who avoid gross sins and indecencies and, when angered, are willing to forgive … Let evil be rewarded with like evil. But he that forgives and seeks reconcilement shall be rewarded by God. He does not love the wrongdoers. Those who seek to redress their wrongs incur no guilt … To endure with fortitude and to forgive is a duty incumbent on all.*
>
> (Qur'an 42:38–43)

Although humans want to be forgiven by people they have wronged, it is the forgiveness of Allah that matters most. By asking people's forgiveness for doing wrong and accepting somebody's request for forgiveness, Muslims will please Allah.

> *Show forgiveness, speak for justice, and avoid the ignorant.* (Qur'an 7:199)

Activity 1

Draw a diagram showing the relationship between the forgiveness of Allah and the way people should forgive each other. Remember it is prohibited in Islam to draw images of Allah and Prophet Muhammed, so try to make your diagram decorative or abstract.

2 The example of Muhammad

The life of Prophet Muhammad offers Muslims many examples of how forgiveness and reconciliation worked at a time when blood feuds and vendettas were common. After Muhammad captured the city of Mecca, its leaders were brought before him and many people expected them to be executed. But Muhammad said, 'You are all free.' By forgiving his enemies, Muhammad turned them into friends and allies, which showed the wisdom of forgiveness and how it could be turned into an act of reconciliation. This also teaches Muslims that showing mercy and forgiveness is not a sign of weakness.

> *Control your anger, then forgive your brother. Do you not wish to be forgiven?* (Prophet Muhammad)

Al-Ghaffar is the fourteenth of the 99 names of Allah and means 'the ever-forgiving'. In the Qur'an, Allah told people, 'He that incurs My wrath shall assuredly be lost, but he that repents and believes in Me, does good works and follows the right path shall be forgiven' (Qur'an 20:82).

3 Teachings about the Day of Judgement

Muslims believe that, after they die, Allah will judge them on the way they have lived their life on earth and whether they have followed the path Allah has set out in the Qur'an. Because Allah is merciful, a person who repents of their sins whilst they are still alive will be forgiven. Because no one knows the time of their death, this means that asking forgiveness should be a normal part of life.

A Muslim is taught to:

- recognise and admit they have made a mistake
- **ask forgiveness from Allah**
- **ask forgiveness from the person themselves**
- try to make up for the wrong they have done someone
- aim not to commit that sin again.

Whilst forgiveness and reconciliation are important virtues, Muslims are taught that, occasionally, forgiveness is not the right response. This is because Muslims have a duty to Allah to protect the religion and the principles it stands for.

> *Don't forgive willfully unjust. If we tolerate wrong by allowing it to run rampant when we can prevent it, we fail in our duty to Allah.*
>
> **(Hadith)**

Muslims stand together on Mount Arafat during Hajj to pray. During this time, they repent of their sins and pray for God's forgiveness.

Activity 2

Muhammad told his followers to "Be forgiving and control yourself in front of provocation". Can you think of a situation where a Muslim could put this advice into practice?

Al-Ghafur is another of the 99 names of Allah and means 'the all-forgiving' and the Qur'an teaches Muslims that 'God is forgiving and merciful' (Qur'an 2:173).

> *Be forgiving and control yourself in front of provocation; give justice to the person who was unfair and unjust to you; give to the one who did not help you when you were in need, and did keep fellowship with the one who did not care about you.*
>
> **(Hadith)**

Check you have learnt:

- three reasons why Muslims should forgive each other
- reasons why reconciliation is important
- what things cannot be forgiven and why.

TRY YOUR SKILL AT THIS

The (c) question:

Explain the importance of forgiveness in **one** religion other than Christianity.

SKILLS COACHING 9

END OF CHAPTER 3 CHECK

Check the (a) question

In this chapter about *Peace and conflict* you have learnt these **KEYWORDS** :

aggression	bullying	conflict resolution	exploitation
forgiveness	just war	pacifism	reconciliation
respect	the United Nations	weapons of mass destruction	world peace

a) Choose three keywords from the list and explain what they mean.

b) Which three keywords did you not want to choose? Write down what you think their meanings might be and check them. Or, if you really don't know, then look them up and write down their meanings. It's better to face the difficult keywords now!

Check the (c) question

Make sure that you understand:
- the work of the United Nations and religious organizations to promote world peace
- why wars occur and the theory of a just war
- Christian and Muslim attitudes to war and their reasons
- Christian and Muslim attitudes to bullying and their reasons
- why religious conflicts might occur in families
- Christian and Muslim attitudes to forgiveness and reconciliation.

Check the (b) and (d) questions

Check you know different people's responses to the issues above for the (b) and (d) questions.

Obviously, your responses to the issues above are the most important ones. Rehearse two or three reasons you would give to support your viewpoint on each issue.

Remind yourself of the two or three reasons the other side gives to argue against you.

Finally, the vitally important thing, what religious viewpoint are you going to use for each issue?

Here is a typical example of how questions about *Peace and conflict* might be presented on the exam paper. Choose one of these questions to work through in exam conditions in order to check your progress.

SECTION 3 – PEACE AND CONFLICT
You must answer ONE question from this section.

EITHER

5 (a) What is **conflict resolution**? (2)

(b) 'Religious people should not fight.'
Do you agree? Give **two** reasons for your point of view. (4)

(c) Explain how the United Nations tries to bring about world peace. (8)

(d) 'If religions practised forgiveness and reconciliation, there wouldn't be any family conflicts.'
In your answer you should refer to at least one religion.
(i) Do you agree? Give reasons for your opinion. (3)
(ii) Give reasons why some people may disagree with you. (3)

(Total for Question 5 = 20 marks)

OR

6 (a) What is meant by **forgiveness**? (2)

(b) 'Religion causes conflicts in families.'
Do you agree? Give **two** reasons for your point of view. (4)

(c) Choose **one** religion other than Christianity and explain its attitude to bullying. (8)

(d) 'War is never just.'
In your answer you should refer to at least one religion.
(i) Do you agree? Give reasons for your opinion. (3)
(ii) Give reasons why some people may disagree with you. (3)

(Total for Question 6 = 20 marks)

If this had been the real exam, how well would you have done? Use the marking grid to check your progress. Answers to (a) appear on page 69, the grid for (b) is on page 31, the grid for (c) is on page 30 and the grid for (d) is on page 31.

CHAPTER 4

Crime and punishment

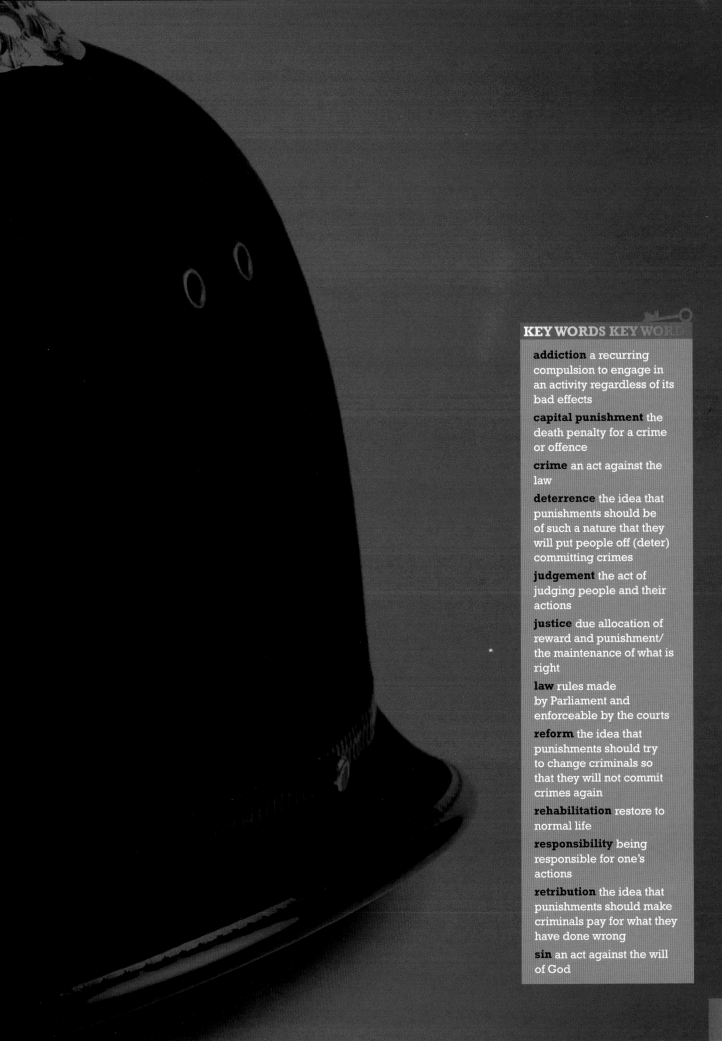

KEY WORDS KEY WORDS

addiction a recurring compulsion to engage in an activity regardless of its bad effects

capital punishment the death penalty for a crime or offence

crime an act against the law

deterrence the idea that punishments should be of such a nature that they will put people off (deter) committing crimes

judgement the act of judging people and their actions

justice due allocation of reward and punishment/ the maintenance of what is right

law rules made by Parliament and enforceable by the courts

reform the idea that punishments should try to change criminals so that they will not commit crimes again

rehabilitation restore to normal life

responsibility being responsible for one's actions

retribution the idea that punishments should make criminals pay for what they have done wrong

sin an act against the will of God

Useful specialist terms

anarchy this is a situation where law and order have completely broken down and normal life is impossible

Activity 1

a) With a partner, list **five** ways in which you think school life would improve if there were no school rules.

b) With the same partner, list **five** ways in which you think school life would become difficult if there were no school rules.

c) Share your ideas with the class.

Do we need laws?

Scenes of rioting and the vandalism of cars and property, like the one on this page, are sufficient to convince most people that a society needs **laws**. Without them, normal daily life breaks down completely, the weak are exploited and the bullies rule. Without any rules, there is anarchy and destruction, civilization breaks down and everything that people have achieved is destroyed.

For rules to be effective, they have to be set up by an authority. In a democratic society like the UK, these rules are agreed by Parliament and called laws. Not only do the laws tell people how they should behave, to be effective there have to be punishments set out for those who break the law.

● Laws tell people how they should and should not behave.

● Laws set out certain punishments to be enforced if the law is broken.

Laws exist so that people know exactly what sort of behaviour is acceptable in their society. With laws in place, people are free to get on with their daily lives. This leads to a civilized society where people can make progress, rather than devoting all their time to protecting their lives and possessions.

What do we mean by justice?

When we talk of **justice**, we generally mean ensuring that people are treated fairly. So, if someone commits a **crime**, there has to be a punishment that is appropriate to the wrong that has been done. If a court sentenced a person to three years' imprisonment for parking on a double yellow line, few would call that justice! Neither would people think justice had been done if a serial rapist was let off with a £100 fine. When we talk of justice, we expect the punishment to be fair and to fit the crime.

Activity 2

For discussion: 'To have freedom, you must have rules.' What do you think?

What is the connection between law and justice?

The statue of justice on the top of the Old Bailey, which is the most important criminal court in the country, shows that British society thinks there clearly is a connection between justice and the law.

The Christian philosopher, Thomas Aquinas, said that laws must be based on justice or they will never work. When people feel a law is unjust, they will take every opportunity to break it. You have only got to think of the way some motorway drivers behave when they think there is no need for a speed restriction on the motorway.

Another danger of having laws that people think are unjust is that they may decide to 'take the law into their own hands' and deal out the punishments they think are right. Law and order rapidly breaks down when the streets are ruled by vigilante groups whose idea of justice is frequently harsh and barbaric.

Activity 3

Create a mind map showing the links between LAW and JUSTICE.

This statue, on the top of the Central Criminal Court at the Old Bailey, symbolizes justice. What does she hold in her hands? Why are scales used as a symbol of justice? Why does she carry a sword? What do you think this is saying about justice?

Check you have learnt:

- three reasons why it is important to have laws
- what is meant by justice
- why law and justice have to be linked.

TRY YOUR SKILL AT THIS

The (c) question:

Explain why society needs both law and justice. (8)

4.2 What is the point of punishment?

In this topic you will study the theories of punishment and the arguments for and against them.

Laws only work if crime is seen to be punished. Here are some of the theories regarding the aims of punishment. Most punishments contain a mixture of these things. One thing everyone agrees on is that the punishment should make criminals take **responsibility** for their actions.

KEYWORDS KEYWORD

responsibility being responsible for one's actions

deterrence the idea that punishments should be of such a nature that they will put people off (deter) committing crimes

retribution the idea that punishments should make criminals pay for what they have done wrong

reform the idea that punishments should try to change criminals so that they will not commit crimes again

rehabilitation restore to normal life

1. Protection

Punishing a wrongdoer by locking them in prison, or taking their life, in order to protect society from the criminal. Does this work as well for a debtor as a child abuser?

2. Deterrent

Having a sufficiently harsh punishment to discourage others from breaking the law. A **deterrent** is also likely to discourage a criminal from re-offending. Would this work for 'crimes of passion' where the husband comes in and finds his wife in bed with another man, then attacks that man?

3. Retribution

Punishing a person in order to make them pay for what they have done. **Retribution** is sometimes summed up as 'an eye for an eye'. Does this punishment work for a person who assists someone with voluntary euthanasia?

4. Reform

A method of punishment that aims to stop a criminal from re-offending. **Reform** can be achieved through a programme of education and training in prison. Will society be content for the unemployed murderer to be enrolled on a course for plumbers?

Activity 1

Create a table or spreadsheet and list each of the five punishment theories. Note down the advantages and disadvantages of each punishment.

5. Reparation

Through punishment, a criminal is made to pay for their crime by doing something to help society or the victim. Once a criminal has settled this debt, they are **rehabilitated** into society and can start life afresh. Is it sufficient for the drink-driver to pay a large fine to the family of the deceased?

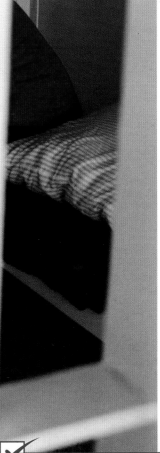

Activity 3

YOB SMASHES PENSIONER'S GREENHOUSE

In court today, Mark Pratt, 14, said he was 'messing about' near the allotments but admitted he was drunk and couldn't remember anything. Eyewitnesses saw him throwing stones at the greenhouse.

YOUNG WOMAN SHOPLIFTER SENTENCED

Paula Simpson, 17, was arrested as she walked out of 'Nightshades' with two designer handbags, worth £265, which she had not paid for. She asked for seven other offences to be taken into consideration.

a) With a partner, choose **one** of the newspaper stories. Taking each of the theories of punishment in turn, decide:

- what punishment should be given for the offence
- whether the punishment would work
- if the punishment is just.

b) As a class, discuss which punishment most people feel would be appropriate for each offence and why.

Check you have learnt:

- how punishments can serve different purposes
- four different theories of punishment
- the strengths and weaknesses of punishments.

TRY YOUR SKILL AT THIS

The (b) question:

'Trying to reform criminals is a waste of time.'

Do you agree? Give **two** reasons for your point of view. (4)

In this topic you will look at Christian beliefs about justice and its importance.

sin an act against the will of God

judgement the act of judging people and their actions

The Bible teaches Christians that God is just and expects his people to treat each other in the same way. Treating people unjustly is a **sin**, and those who do it can expect to pay the price on the Day of **Judgement**.

The Old Testament idea of justice was one of retribution. In the book of Exodus it states: '… the punishment shall be life for life, eye for eye, tooth for tooth' and it continues down to 'bruise for bruise' (Exodus 21:23–5). What the Old Testament also made clear was that once the punishment was given, no more could be taken. Vendettas and long-running disputes were unjust.

MEEK MILD AS IF
Discover the real Jesus

Although Christians think of Jesus as the 'Prince of Peace', the Gospels also show that he was not prepared to sit back and allow injustices to happen.

Jesus' teachings about justice

Jesus' teachings about justice were revolutionary for the time, and are still something many Christians struggle to accept today. Jesus linked justice with non-violence and forgiveness. He taught his followers that retribution was not the best way, but that they should use love to overcome injustice. Forgiving a person who has hurt you, he said, was better than exacting punishment.

> *Do not judge others, so that God will not judge you, for God will judge you in the same way as you judge others, and he will apply to you the same rules you apply to others.*
> **(Matthew 7:1–2)**

> *You have heard that it was said, "An eye for an eye, and a tooth for a tooth." But now I tell you: do not take revenge on someone who wrongs you. If anyone slaps you on the right cheek, let him slap your left cheek too.*
> **(Matthew 5:38–9)**

Some Christians tackle the injustice of poverty in less economically developed countries by purchasing Fairtrade goods. This ensures that those who made the goods receive a just price for their work.

Fighting injustice

Through his teachings and by example, Jesus explained to his followers how they could bring about the just society that God requires. Jesus taught people to share their wealth with those who have nothing, to create a fairer and just society. This has led some Christians to give money to charity and to take part in projects to share the earth's resources more fairly.

Modern Christians also believe that there is an unjust division of wealth in the world and they campaign against poverty in less economically developed countries. 'Make Poverty History' and 'Drop the Debt' are some of the campaigns they actively support.

In addition to protesting about unfair trading terms and putting pressure on the government to help the poor, some Christians make a deliberate effort to purchase Fairtrade goods. By doing so, the growers and suppliers are guaranteed a fair price for their goods, which enables them to educate their children and improve their standard of living. This is in contrast to the way some large supermarket chains use their might to force suppliers in less economically developed countries to sell things at the lowest price possible. Whilst this maximizes the supermarket's profits and gives consumers cheap food, it forces the growers to remain in poverty.

> *He has sent me to proclaim liberty to the captives and recovery of sight to the blind; to set free the oppressed and announce that the time has come when the Lord will save his people.*
> **(Luke 4:18–19)**

Activity 1

Jesus' message is often referred to as 'turning the other cheek'. Read the quotation from Matthew 5:38–9 and explain what it means. How could it work?

Activity 2

a) Visit the Fairtrade Foundation website and make a list of **ten** products that they sell.

b) Choose **one** product and find out about the producer. Write a magazine article explaining how choosing a Fairtrade product helps someone.

Activity 3

Role-play an interview between a cocoa grower, who is forced to sell his produce to a supermarket at less than it costs him to produce it, and the supermarket owner, who is a churchgoer.

Check you have learnt:

- reasons why Christians think injustice is a sin
- what Jesus taught his followers about injustice
- two ways in which Christians fight injustice.

TRY YOUR SKILL AT THIS

The (c) question:

Explain why justice is important to Christians. (8)

Why is justice important to Muslims?

In this topic you will look at Muslim beliefs about justice and its importance.

Useful specialist terms

Shari'ah Law this is a code of law based on the teachings of the Qur'an and the practice of the prophet Muhammad

zakah a Muslim gives 2.5% of their spare income to help others; this is a way of spreading wealth more justly between people

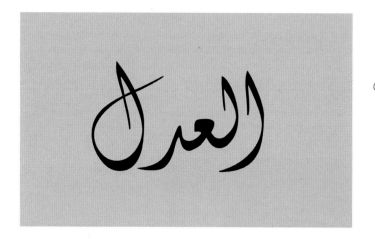

One of the 99 names of Allah is Al-'Adl, which means 'The Just'. This shows Muslims how important justice is.

Allah is just

Justice is extremely important to Muslims because they believe that Allah is just. He created everybody equal and treats his creation with justice and fairness. Allah expects everyone to treat each other in the same way.

Those who do not treat other people with justice will be judged accordingly when they go before Allah on the Day of Judgement. If they have not shown mercy to others, they cannot expect Allah to show mercy to them. On the Day of Judgement, the good will be rewarded and the evil punished; that is the justice of Allah.

Muslims believe that they have a duty to work towards a just society and the Qur'an gives them guidance.

> *Those who seek to redress their wrongs incur no guilt. But great is the guilt of those who oppress their fellow men and conduct themselves with wickedness and injustice in the land. They shall be sternly punished.* **(Qur'an 42:40)**

> *Believers, conduct yourselves with justice and bear true witness before God.* **(Qur'an 4:135)**

Many aspects of Islamic life centre on the idea of a just society. Here are three of them:

- **Shari'ah law** – Muslims are taught that it is Allah's will that they should follow the straight path of life set out in the Qur'an. The Islam legal system is called Shari'ah Law. It is based on the idea of justice for everyone and it puts the teachings of the Qur'an into laws. All Muslims are entitled to equal treatment under Shari'ah Law. Islamic courts use Shari'ah Law to decide on just punishments if the laws of Allah are broken.

- **Zakah** – this is the third pillar of Islam. It requires a Muslim to share out 2.5% of their surplus income amongst people less fortunate than themselves. Muslims regard this as simple justice because it is working towards a more equal society.

- **It is unjust to charge interest** – Muslims are taught that everyone has a duty to treat each other fairly. Those who have money should help those who do not have money. The Qur'an teaches that it is unjust for someone to loan money to another person and charge them interest because that only makes the rich person richer and the poor person poorer. Muslims try to use an Islamic Bank for their savings, so that any money earned goes to help those who are less fortunate. Some UK high-street banks, like HSBC, have a special account so Muslims can obey Shari'ah Law.

Activity 1

Explain what Muslims mean when they say Allah is just.

Activity 2

Write a brief explanation for a new bank employee to help them understand why a Muslim would not want to use one of the bank's ordinary savings accounts.

Water & Sanitation

Islamic Relief delivering water in the Somali region of Ethiopia.

Prophet Muhammad, peace be upon him, said the best form of charity is to provide water.

www.islamic-relief.org.uk

Reg Charity No. 328158

By donating to the work of a Muslim charity like Islamic Relief, Muslims are working for justice and equality in the world.

Activity 3

Make notes on the reasons why Muslims believe justice is important and the actions they take to create a fairer society.

 Check you have learnt:

- reasons why Muslims believe justice matters
- three ways in which Muslims fight injustice
- what the Qur'an teaches Muslims about justice.

TRY YOUR SKILL AT THIS

The (d) question:

'Justice is more important to religious believers than to non-religious people.'

In your answer you should refer to one religion.

(i) Do you agree? Give reasons for your opinion.

(ii) Give reasons why some people may disagree with you.

Working for a just society

In addition to paying zakah, Muslims are encouraged to work towards making society fairer. This might take the form of donating money to a charity like Islamic Relief or recycling clothes in one of their clothing banks. If suitable, the clothes are given to the needy or they may be sold to raise money to help those who are less fortunate.

Some Muslims actively campaign for a just society and regularly join non-Muslims on marches like 'Make Poverty History'. The aim is to draw people's attention to the unequal division of the earth's resources and to pressure the government to assist less economically developed countries.

SKILLS COACHING 10

DO YOU KNOW?

Improve your skill with the (a) question

Write out the meaning of each of these **KEYWORDS** from memory:

justice
(page 100)

law
(page 100)

crime
(page 100)

sin
(page 104)

deterrence
(page 102)

reform
(page 102)

retribution
(page 102)

responsibility
(page 102)

rehabilitation
(page 102)

judgement
(page 104)

Check back in the section and mark your answers according to the mark scheme on page 30.

> **✳ TRY THIS ✳**
>
> Work with a partner and each select four keywords and meanings from earlier chapters in this textbook. Make them difficult! In fact, choose the four that you found hardest to remember because, by doing so, it will help you to fix their meanings in your mind. Now challenge your partner to give you the correct definition. Swap round and see who wins. You can play it as a class game if you prefer.

Improve your skill with the (c) question

Check you understand the different ways in which punishments can be used and the advantages and disadvantages of these reasons for punishment. Do you understand the way justice and law are connected? Revise the reasons why Christians and Muslims believe justice is important.

> Explain why justice is important in **one** *religion other than Christianity.* (8)

Remember the step by step approach?

STEP 1

Underline the important words in the question. Write down the name of the religion you are going to write about. It will be Islam.

STEP 2

Jot down as many points as you can think of.

STEP 3

Write up each point as a full sentence with a good developed reason or some briefer reasons. One paragraph for each point.

Complete Paula's answer below. Aim for a Level 4 response.

> Muslims think justice is extremely important because Allah is just. This means that if people don't treat each other justly, then Allah will judge them. This is likely to mean that they will go to hell. There are lots of things Muslims do to be just – one of them is called zakah.

Swap your answer with a partner and use the grid on page 30 to mark each other's response. Put a helpful comment at the end of the answer.

WHAT DO YOU THINK?

Improve your skill with the (d) question

The (d) question starts by asking you for your views; then goes further and asks for the opposite view. Remember that you have to include the response of **one** of the religions you have studied, so tell the examiner clearly. A good way is to start with *'Some Christians would say …'* or *'Many Muslims think …'*. This leaves it open for you to offer another viewpoint from that religion, and the examiner is very clear which religion you are writing about.

'Having laws takes away people's freedom.'

'Reform is the best sort of punishment.'

'An eye for an eye is the fairest punishment.'

Choose one of the quotations above to answer. The question will go on to ask:

In your answer you should refer to at least one religion.
(i) Do you agree? Give reasons for your opinion. (3)
(ii) Give reasons why some people may disagree with you. (3)

Dipesh decided to answer the question 'Reform is the best sort of punishment.' Here is his answer along with the examiner's marks:

(i) Well, I don't agree with that at all because if you were the victim, you would feel let down if your attacker spent all his time on an education course. ✓ (1 mark for good reason) The punishment has got to fit the crime. ✓ (1 mark for another brief reason) I think the criminal has got to be made to suffer so he doesn't do it again. ✓ (1 mark for an expanded reason)

(ii) On the other hand, if you do reform them, the criminal won't do it again. ✓ (1 mark for a brief reason) This means that we will all be safer and that's a good reason. ✓ (1 mark for an expanded reason) Some Christians would agree with me because Jesus taught them that they should forgive people who hurt them and, if you try and reform someone, well, I think that is forgiving them. You are helping them to make a fresh start. ✓ (1 mark)

Below is the start of Vikki's answer to the question: 'Having laws takes away people's freedom.' As you can see, she has managed **two** brief reasons in part (i). Complete part (i) to gain another mark, then write an answer to part (ii) to gain the full 3 marks.

(i) I think all the rules they have these days are no good, they stop you doing what you want to and everybody should be allowed to do what they want. ✓ (1 mark) You don't need rules to tell you not to steal, we all know that is wrong. And, anyway, if you have too many rules, people don't take much notice of them do they? Rules that say it is wrong to drive at 31mph when it is okay to do 30mph are silly. You should be trusted to do the right thing. ✓ (Just about given another reason after a long ramble – 1 mark)

In this topic you will examine the nature of capital punishment and evaluate the reasons for and against it.

KEYWORDS KEYWORD

capital punishment the death penalty for a crime or offence

In 2000, Dr Harold Shipman was convicted of killing 15 patients. An enquiry concluded the number could be closer to 250. Shipman was sentenced to prison for the rest of his life, but he committed suicide in 2004.

Activity 1

a) What arguments could be put forward to support the death penalty for Harold Shipman, the UK's worst serial killer?

b) Would you have supported the death penalty for Harold Shipman? Why?

What is capital punishment?

Capital punishment means using execution as the punishment for a crime or offence. Only the State or a recognised authority can do this after they have held a proper trial. Anyone else who executes a person is committing murder.

Capital punishment is still used legally in 71 countries around the world, but the UN is working towards its abolition. In the UK, the last person to be executed was in 1964; the death penalty was finally abolished for all crimes in the UK in 1998. However, the reintroduction of the death penalty is regularly discussed for crimes such as murdering a policeman.

A few facts from AMNESTY INTERNATIONAL

2390 people were put to death in 2008, up from 1252 in 2007. A further 8864 people were sentenced to death in 2008.

Amnesty's figures show that China executed 1718 people in 2008 which is 72% of the total number of people put to death in the year. This figure represents a minimum estimate – the real figure is undoubtedly higher.

Iran has the second-highest figure for executions; in 2008 they recorded 346 deaths, including eight juveniles.

The six countries with the highest execution figures are China (at least 1718), Iran (at least 346), Saudi Arabia (at least 102), USA (37), Pakistan (at least 36) and Iraq (at least 34).

36 American states have the death penalty. Nine of these states carried out executions in 2008, and just under half of the executions that took place in America in 2008 were carried out in Texas.

The only country in Europe that still executes prisoners is Belarus.

Those in favour of capital punishment say:

- It is an excellent deterrent. Knowing that they could be executed for a crime is likely to stop most people committing it in the first place.
- The death penalty removes dangerous people, like terrorists and serial killers, from society, making it a safer place for us all. It certainly stops re-offending.
- The death penalty is far cheaper than keeping a criminal in a maximum security prison for the rest of their life at the State's expense.
- A life for a life is fair retribution. Human life is the most valuable thing a person has, so a murderer should lose theirs.
- The death penalty gives the victim's family a sense of closure, which helps them to get on with their lives.

Those against capital punishment say:

- Innocent people get convicted by mistake; using the death penalty prevents mistakes being corrected.
- Life is sacred; no one has the right to kill another person.
- Life in prison is a greater deterrent to many criminals, which is why some try to commit suicide.
- If there is a death penalty for murder, there is nothing to stop a person killing many people.
- The death penalty is inhuman and barbaric; it creates a brutal society.
- A UN survey in 1988 and 1996 found no evidence that capital punishment was a deterrent.
- Terrorists are sometimes regarded as heroes or martyrs, which might encourage others to follow.

Amnesty International opposes the death penalty in all circumstances because it is a violation of two fundamental human rights, as laid down in Articles 3 and 5 of the Universal Declaration of Human Rights:

- The right to life.
- The right not to be tortured or subjected to any cruel, inhuman or degrading punishment.

The death penalty is the ultimate cruel, inhuman and degrading punishment. It is irrevocable and can be inflicted on the innocent. It has never been shown to deter crime more effectively than other punishments.

Activity 2

a) Look back to the theories of punishment on pages 102–103. Read through each one and decide whether capital punishment fits the criteria. Share your conclusions with the class.

b) Take a class vote on whether the death penalty should be reinstated in the UK.

 Check you have learnt:

- what capital punishment means
- four reasons to support capital punishment
- four reasons to oppose capital punishment.

CASE STUDY

In London in 1953, Derek Bentley, aged 19, was hanged for the murder of a policeman in a robbery that went wrong. The shot that killed the policeman was fired by Chris Craig, his accomplice, who was aged 16. Both were found guilty of murder, but Craig went to prison because he was underage. Bentley was sentenced to death because he was alleged to have told Craig to 'Let him have it'. Bentley had learning difficulties and a mental age of 11. In 1998, the Court of Appeal overturned Bentley's conviction for murder. Craig served ten years in prison and has remained out of trouble ever since.

Activity 3

a) Why was the case of Derek Bentley controversial?

b) What does it add to the debate about capital punishment?

TRY YOUR SKILL AT THIS

The (d) question:

'Capital punishment can never be fair.'

(i) Do you agree? Give reasons for your opinion. (3)

(ii) Give reasons why some people may disagree with you. (3)

In this topic you will consider the different attitudes Christians have towards capital punishment and their reasons.

Because Jesus suffered the death penalty for crimes he did not commit, some Christians hold strong views against capital punishment.

Activity 1

MEMO

From: PJY Productions

Re: **Tell the World**

On Sunday morning's chat show, **Tell the World**, we have got Lucia Benedit, a leading Christian supporter of capital punishment. Chas is hosting the show and wants some info on what Lucia is likely to say. Can you note down a few points, along with two challenging questions Chas can put to her?

Whilst all Christians agree that human life is sacred and killing is wrong, some make an exception when it comes to taking a life in war or as punishment for crime.

The Bible leads some Christians to support capital punishment

The Old Testament has many teachings about the death penalty, and Christians who accept the Bible as the Word of God use this to justify their belief in capital punishment.

> *If anyone takes human life, he will be punished … Human beings were made like God, so whoever murders one of them will be killed by someone else.*
> **(Genesis 9:5–6)**

The sixth of the Ten Commandments God gave to Moses says 'Do not commit murder'. This leads some Christians to believe that it is such a serious crime, therefore capital punishment is justified.

In the New Testament, St Paul told Christians:

> *Everyone must obey the state authorities, because no authority exists without God's permission, and the existing authorities have been put there by God.*
> **(Romans 13:1)**

This means that if capital punishment is part of a country's legal code, Christians must obey the law. Jesus also taught his followers that they must do what the law demands of them, whether it is the law of the State or religious rules.

Jesus told his followers: 'Whoever curses his father or his mother is to be put to death' (Matthew 15:4).

The Christian Church has a tradition of using the death penalty as a punishment for heresy.

Christians who support the death penalty would also use the non-religious reasons given on pages 110–111 to justify their case.

The reasons why other Christians are against capital punishment

● Jesus' message was one of love and compassion. He emphasized the importance of forgiveness rather than retribution.

● On several occasions Jesus said that he had come to save sinners, but if the state executes a criminal, there is no chance for Christians to save them from their sins or help them to reform their behaviour.

● Passages in the Bible teach Christians that only God can give life and only God can take it away. This does not permit anyone, or any authority, to execute a person. Christians regularly use these teachings to forbid abortion and euthanasia, which leads some to argue that they must also apply to the death penalty.

● The Old Testament punishments may have been appropriate for an ancient society, but today's society has different attitudes and other ways of dealing with offenders.

● For some Christians, the sixth commandment means that no one is permitted to kill anybody.

● There is evidence that some people who have suffered the death penalty in the past were mentally ill, or trapped in a life of crime and poverty where they had little choice. Jesus came to save people like this and Christians believe it is their duty to do the same.

Read the Roman Catholic Church's statement about capital punishment:

> *Assuming that the guilty party's identity and responsibility have been fully determined, the traditional teaching of the Church does not exclude recourse to the death penalty, if this is the only possible way of effectively defending human lives against the unjust aggressor. If, however, non-lethal means are sufficient to defend and protect people's safety from the aggressor, authority will limit itself to such means, as these are more in keeping with the concrete conditions of the common good and are more in conformity to the dignity of the human person. … The cases in which the execution of the offender is an absolute necessity are very rare, if not practically non-existent.* **(Catechism of the Catholic Church 2267)**

This is death row in the state of California in America. Some Christians who disagree with capital punishment visit the inmates to bring them comfort.

Activity 2

Using a spreadsheet or table, record the arguments Christians might use for and against capital punishment. Don't forget to include the non-religious points on page 111.

 Check you have learnt:

● three reasons why some Christians support capital punishment

● three reasons why other Christians are against capital punishment.

Activity 3

Analyse this statement by the Roman Catholic Church.

a) Does it permit capital punishment?

b) What other points does it make about the death penalty?

c) Would you say these Christians were in favour of the death penalty? Explain your answer.

TRY YOUR SKILL AT THIS

The (c) question:

Explain why Christians disagree over capital punishment. (8)

In this topic you will consider the different attitudes Muslims have towards capital punishment and their reasons.

Useful specialist terms

apostasy when a Muslim denies their religion and actively works against it

> *You shall not kill any man whom God has forbidden you to kill, except for a just cause.*
>
> **(Qur'an 17:33)**

Justice is most important

Islam is a religion that is based on peace and justice. For some crimes, Muslims believe that death is a just punishment. To let someone off would be an injustice for the victim and their family, it would also be damaging to society. Although society must punish a criminal for their behaviour, Muslims believe that Allah will be the ultimate judge and he will punish them in the afterlife.

Islam regards the death penalty as the correct form of retribution for some crimes. Capital punishment is also regarded as a deterrent and a punishment that safeguards people's lives and property.

For capital punishment to be legal, the accused must be given a fair trial in a court of law and found guilty. Other less severe punishments are also possible under Shari'ah Law and these must be weighed up against the crime. However, in the most severe cases, capital punishment is believed to be the just punishment.

> *... Whoever killed a human being, except as punishment for murder or other villainy in the land, shall be deemed as though he had killed all mankind; and that whoever saved a human life shall be deemed as though he had saved all mankind.*
>
> **(Qur'an 5:32)**

> *... You shall not kill – for that is forbidden by God – except for a just cause.*
>
> **(Qur'an 6:151)**

Activity 1

Explain how the death penalty could be seen as a just punishment. You might find it helpful to give an example.

Shari'ah Law permits the death penalty for:

- **deliberate murder**. The family of a victim has the right to say whether or not they wish the murderer to be executed.
- **threatening to undermine the authority**. This is a wide area, which is interpreted in different ways that range from treason and terrorism to adultery and homosexuality. It also includes apostasy, when a Muslim rejects their religion and actively works against it.

Not all Muslims demand the death penalty

Some Muslims point out that the Qur'an does permit other punishments. For instance, the family of a victim is permitted to pardon the criminal and accept a payment of 'blood money' rather than insist on execution. Whilst all Muslim countries have the death penalty on their statute books, some countries have not used it for many years.

Islam permits the death penalty to be carried out by firing squad, beheading, hanging or stoning.

> ### Activity 2
>
> For discussion: Is it a good idea to let a victim's family decide on the right punishment? Why? Note down the points given for and against this.

> ✓ **Check you have learnt:**
>
> - the Muslim attitude to capital punishment
> - the two categories of crime that warrant capital punishment
> - whether all Muslims agree with capital punishment.

> **TRY YOUR SKILL AT THIS**
>
> **The (c) question:**
>
> Explain why followers of **one** *religion other than Christianity* believe in capital punishment. (8)

DO YOU KNOW?

Improve your skill with the (a) question

These **KEYWORDS** have occurred in Chapter 4 so far.

capital punishment
(page 110)

retribution
(page 102)

deterrence
(page 102)

responsibility
(page 102)

crime
(page 100)

✳ TRY THIS ✳

Match the meanings to the keywords.

? = an act against the law.

? = the idea that punishments should make criminals pay for what they have done wrong.

? = the death penalty for a crime or offence.

? = being responsible for one's actions.

? = the idea that punishments should be of such a nature that they will put people off (deter) committing crimes.

Improve your skill with the (c) question

Many topics you study in Religious Studies are concerned with religious responses to different issues, but they may also contain material that involves citizenship. Here, you have considered the way people approach justice and punishment. A (c) question will want to discover how much you understand about the reasons why people choose certain responses to crime, and what they are aiming for with that response.

Here are two typical non-religious (c) questions you could be asked:

Explain why punishment is needed. (8)

Explain why some people agree with capital punishment and some do not. (8)

Choose one of these questions to answer. You will notice that the second question is asking for two opposing viewpoints. In this type of question you will need to give both sides of the argument to access the highest level.

When you have completed your answer, swap with a partner and use the marking scheme to award each other marks. How did you do?

Level 1	● One brief reason. ● Not explaining but describing the issue.	1–2 marks
Level 2	● Two brief reasons. ● One expanded reason.	3–4 marks
Level 3	● Three brief reasons. ● One fully-developed reason. ● Two reasons with one expanded.	5–6 marks
Level 4	● Four brief reasons. ● Two expanded reasons. ● Three reasons with one expanded.	7–8 marks

WHAT DO YOU THINK?

Improve your skill with the (b) question

Try out your skills on this (b) question:

'If you believe in justice then capital punishment is right for murder.'

Do you agree? Give **two** reasons for your point of view. (4)

Remember the step-by-step approach?

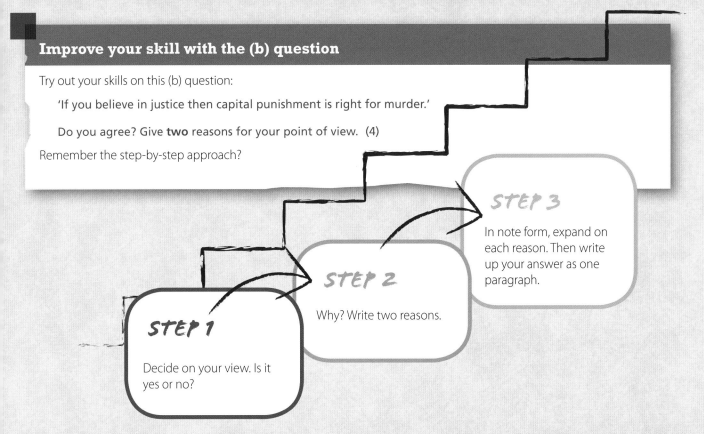

STEP 3

In note form, expand on each reason. Then write up your answer as one paragraph.

STEP 2

Why? Write two reasons.

STEP 1

Decide on your view. Is it yes or no?

Improve your skill with the (d) question

Remember to use a similar approach for the (d) question. Once you have planned out your view, do the same for the opposite view and make this a separate paragraph.

Try this (d) question:

'Capital punishment can never be justified.'

In your answer you should refer to at least one religion.

(i) Do you agree? Give reasons for your opinion. (3)

(ii) Give reasons why some people may disagree with you. (3)

> **! A tip:**
> Is there a religious viewpoint you could include as part of one side of the answer?

In this topic you will study the laws on drugs and alcohol and consider the reasons for those laws.

WHAT IS THE LAW ON ALCOHOL?

⊘ It is illegal to give a child under five an alcoholic drink, except under medical supervision in an emergency.　**WHY?**

⊘ Under 16s cannot drink alcohol in a pub, but they are allowed to go anywhere in a pub so long as they are supervised.
　WHY?

⊘ Young people aged 16 or 17 can drink beer, wine or cider with a meal if it is bought by an adult and they are accompanied by an adult. It is illegal for 16 and 17 year-olds to drink spirits in a pub or with a meal.　**WHY?**

⊘ Nobody under the age of 18 can buy alcohol in a pub, off-licence, supermarket or other outlet. Nobody is allowed to buy alcohol in a pub or public place for under 18s to drink.
　WHY?

Activity 1

Read through the points on the noticeboard giving details of the law about alcohol. Answer the WHY question for each point.

Is the law strong enough?

At the end of 2008, government advisors were urging the government to tighten the laws on alcohol in order to curb the problems of binge drinking. Here are some of their recommendations:

- Ban alcohol adverts on television between 6pm and 9pm.
- Increase the rate of tax as the drink gets stronger.
- Stop the 'happy hour' and prevent supermarkets discounting alcohol.
- Ban the sale of high-strength beer in public places.
- Zero drink-drive limit for under-21s.
- Put a health warning on bottles and adverts.

What does the law say about drugs?

Illegal drugs are divided into three categories:

Class A – includes opium, morphine, heroin, methadone, dextromoramide, cocaine, ecstasy and LSD. Some Class B drugs, such as speed prepared for injection, are also included.

Class B – includes codeine, amphetamine, methylamphetamine, barbiturates and dihydrocodeine.

Class C – includes Ketamine, GHB, cannabis and mainly prescribed drugs such as tranquillisers.

Parliament has passed several laws to prevent the misuse of drugs:

● The police have the power to stop and search anyone, or their vehicle, if the possession of drugs is suspected. The police can seize anything that appears to be illegal and they can arrest anyone suspected of committing an offence.

● It is illegal to be in possession of a controlled drug, but if it can be proved that a drug was put in someone's pocket without their knowledge, it is not an offence.

● It is a serious offence to supply drugs or intend to supply them. This includes giving as well as selling drugs to someone.

● Growing cannabis is a serious offence, especially if it is proved that the drug was intended to supply others.

● Importing and exporting drugs carries heavy penalties.

DON'T LET DRUG DEALERS CHANGE THE FACE OF YOUR NEIGHBOURHOOD.
Call Crimestoppers anonymously on 0800 555 111.

Activity 2

a) With a partner, discuss the ways alcohol laws might be tightened.

b) Which **two** laws do you think would help to prevent binge drinking?

c) Why do you think many of the laws target young people?

Activity 3

Make a poster aimed at informing teenagers about the law on drugs.

 Check you have learnt:

● what the law about alcohol is for your age group

● three illegal aspects of drug possession.

TRY YOUR SKILL AT THIS

The (c) question:
Explain why there are laws to stop children drinking. (8)

In this topic you will examine the social problems and the health problems caused by drugs and alcohol.

KEYWORDS KEYWORD

addiction a recurring compulsion to engage in an activity regardless of its bad effects

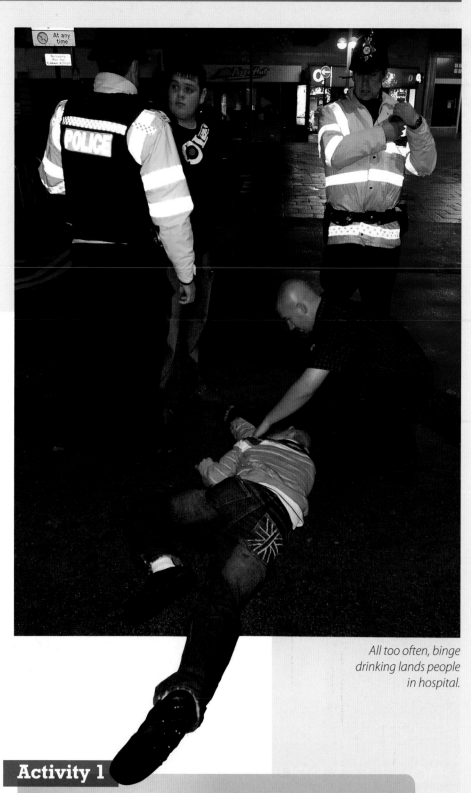

All too often, binge drinking lands people in hospital.

People often think that binge drinking is simply a young person's night out. They say it doesn't mean someone is an alcoholic because they don't drink every night and they keep within the government's safe weekly limit. But consuming the whole weekly limit on one very boozy Saturday night can actually be extremely harmful.

Some facts and figures

- 25% of hospital admissions are alcohol related.
- 40% of domestic violence involves alcohol.
- 33,000 people die each year from alcohol-related causes.
- 19% of men and 5% of women in the UK report having a drink problem.
- Alcohol abuse costs British industry £2 billion through absenteeism or poor work performance.
- 11 people are killed every week in road accidents related to drink.
- 33% of child abuse cases involve alcohol.

Activity 1

Study the facts and figures then write a piece for local radio explaining how alcohol abuse affects far more than the drinker.

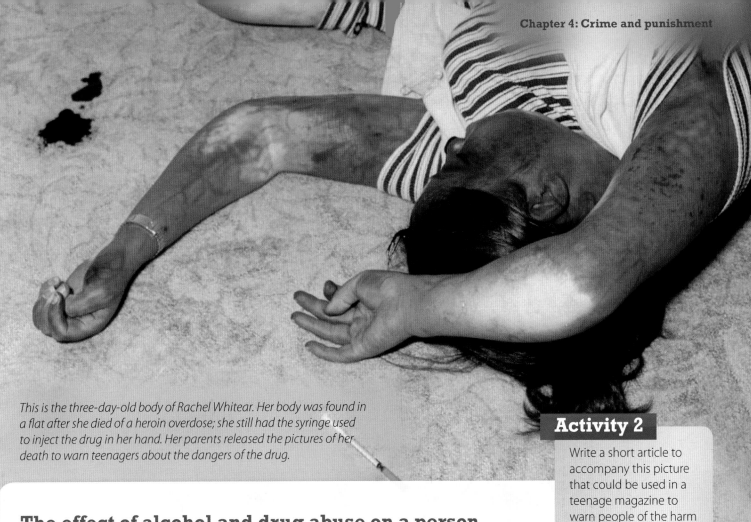

This is the three-day-old body of Rachel Whitear. Her body was found in a flat after she died of a heroin overdose; she still had the syringe used to inject the drug in her hand. Her parents released the pictures of her death to warn teenagers about the dangers of the drug.

The effect of alcohol and drug abuse on a person

- **Accidents happen** – as the picture opposite and statistics show, somebody who is drunk or under the influence of drugs is far more likely to harm themselves or others, especially if they are driving.

- **Crime occurs** – drinkers and drug users are more likely to be the victims of crimes or the cause of violence. Fifty per cent of street crime is related to drink.

- **The person looks terrible** – this may seem the least of their worries but alcohol causes dehydration, which soon shows up on the face. Drug users look even worse as the picture on page 119 shows.

- **Causes health problems** – liver damage is one well-known effect of heavy drinking and it is irreversible. Equally, heart rates and blood pressure rises lead to long-term heart damage. Drugs steadily destroy people's vital organs, as well as causing permanent damage to the brain.

- **Leads to addiction** – alcohol is as much a drug as heroin is and people become addicted. Without medical help and treatment for rehabilitation, people are trapped by their habit.

- **Relationships fail** – partners and families frequently find they are no longer able to deal with an addict who lies to them and treats them badly.

- **Costs a fortune** – feeding a drink or drug habit gets people into debt, which brings its own problems.

- **Work or education suffer** – not only do alcohol or drugs impair someone's mental abilities, addicts often find the only thing they can think about is getting their next fix of drink or drugs.

What is drug misuse?

The drug advisor at 'Release' says that drug misuse is 'when the drugs use you rather than you use them'. What does he mean? Would you agree with this?

Activity 2

Write a short article to accompany this picture that could be used in a teenage magazine to warn people of the harm drugs can do.

Activity 3

Make a leaflet for pupils in Year 7, explaining why there are strict laws about alcohol and drugs.

✓ **Check you have learnt:**

- what is meant by drug and alcohol abuse
- how drug and alcohol abuse harms the person themselves
- how drug and alcohol abuse harms society.

TRY YOUR SKILL AT THIS

The (c) question:

Explain why drug abuse is a serious concern for everybody. (8)

121

What do Christians think about drugs and alcohol?

In this topic you will examine the different attitudes Christians have to drugs and alcohol.

Is it okay to drink?

Christians have different attitudes to the consumption of alcohol. Many accept that alcohol can be enjoyed in a responsible way because there is evidence that Jesus drank wine. The story of the Wedding at Cana tells of Jesus attending a celebration where the wine had run out. His first miracle was to turn the water into wine so the guests could continue celebrating.

As a Jew, Jesus would also have drunk wine as a traditional way of welcoming in the Sabbath. At the Last Supper, Jesus shared wine with his followers and instructed them to do this in the future to remember him.

This leads Catholics and Anglicans to accept that alcohol is not a problem, but drunkenness is because it causes suffering. They accept the use of alcohol as a part of normal life and, in obedience to Jesus' command, wine is at the centre of the Holy Communion service. Wine is a symbol of the blood Jesus shed when he died on the cross to save his followers.

Some Nonconformist churches worked in the slums in Victorian times and saw the misery alcohol abuse caused people. This led leaders of the Methodist Church and Salvation Army to decide that their members should abstain from alcohol completely. They use non-alcoholic wine for the celebration of Holy Communion.

The Salvation Army says:

> *Accepting that alcohol, tobacco and other addictive drugs can be harmful, and can also have consequent effects on individuals, families and society, members of the Salvation Army freely and willingly refrain from the use of these substances in their own lives.*

The Bible teaches Christians that they are made in the image of God, so this leads them to understand that it is wrong to harm their body by alcohol or substance abuse:

> *Don't you know that your body is the temple of the Holy Spirit, who lives in you and who was given to you by God?* **(1 Corinthians 6:19)**

Wine plays an important symbolic role in the Communion service. It represents the blood Jesus shed to save humanity.

Activity 1

Use the Bible quote and the Salvation Army's statement to write a brief newspaper article explaining why some Christians do not drink alcohol.

Activity 2

Make a spider diagram with the extract 1 Corinthians 6:19 in the centre. Show how this affects Christian attitudes to alcohol and drug abuse.

Christian attitudes to drugs

Whilst most Christians accept the use of prescription drugs to make them better, they do not agree with the use of drugs for recreation. Drugs as medicine are a good thing because they relieve suffering, but any other use is forbidden because it causes harm. The biblical teaching 1 Corinthians 6:19 would also apply.

The Methodist Church says:

 Christians must face serious scientific evidence about the harmful effects of drugs. A Christian's faith teaches him to use all things responsibly.
(Methodist Conference)

Helping the addicts

Christians take their lead from Jesus who showed love and compassion for those who were suffering. Members of the Salvation Army and other Christian groups work with people who are addicted to drugs or alcohol. They assist them with medical treatment and help them to work their way through their addiction. There are many rehabilitation centres funded by different Christian organizations. They believe that helping people to get off drugs or alcohol addiction is a form of healing and making the body whole again.

Other Christians work to remove the social conditions that can lead to alcohol or drug dependency.

Greig House is a detoxification centre in East London run by The Salvation Army. The centre is for men and women seeking help with an addiction to drugs and/or alcohol. The treatment provides medical care to help alleviate the physical and mental symptoms of withdrawal and is supported by counselling and group work with educational, motivational and spiritual themes. Greig House aims to help people move towards long-term recovery from substance misuse.

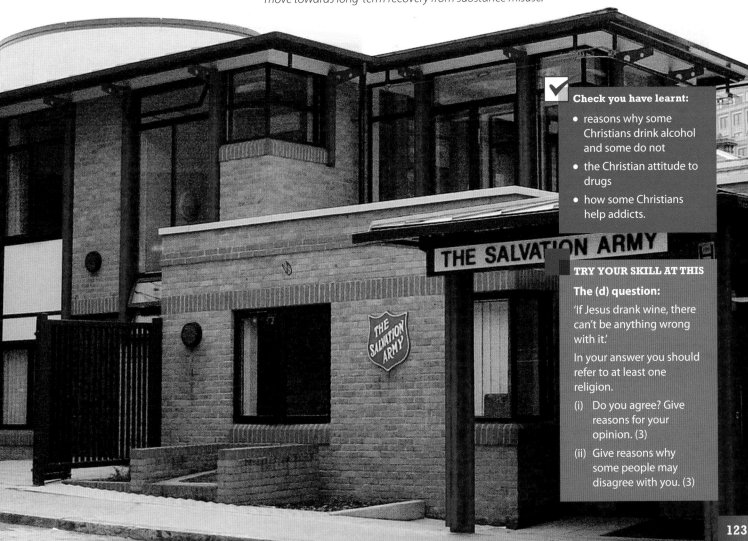

Activity 3

a) Using the Internet, look up Yeldall Manor, a rehabilitation centre run by Christians for men with drug or alcohol addiction. Find out how these Christians help people to get free of their addiction.

b) Give a presentation to the class on the work of this charity.

✔ **Check you have learnt:**

- reasons why some Christians drink alcohol and some do not
- the Christian attitude to drugs
- how some Christians help addicts.

TRY YOUR SKILL AT THIS

The (d) question:

'If Jesus drank wine, there can't be anything wrong with it.'

In your answer you should refer to at least one religion.

(i) Do you agree? Give reasons for your opinion. (3)

(ii) Give reasons why some people may disagree with you. (3)

What do Muslims think about drugs and alcohol?

In this topic you will examine the Muslim attitude to drugs and alcohol.

Useful specialist terms

haram something that is totally forbidden in Islam

Islam treats the subject of alcohol and drug abuse very seriously. Taking alcohol or drugs is haram – totally forbidden by the Qu'ran. Both are intoxicants that can lead to addiction. They destroy a person's body, which no one has a right to damage because Allah is the owner of our bodies. Not only individuals, but families and society, are hurt by substance abuse.

The Qur'an says:

> *Believers, do not approach your prayers when you are drunk, but wait till you can grasp the meaning of your words.* **(Qur'an 4:43)**

> *Satan stirs up hatred among you by means of wine and gambling … Will you not abstain from them?* **(Qur'an 5:90)**

> *They ask you about drinking and gambling. Say: "There is great harm in both, although they have some benefit for men; but their harm is far greater than their benefit."* **(Qur'an 2:219)**

Muhammad said:

> *Intoxicants are the mother of all evils.*
> *Alcohol is not a medicine but a disease.*

Islam aims to create a peaceful and just society. Alcoholism and drug addiction are evil because they destroy society. Because some people find it far too easy to slip from a small drink into full-scale addiction, Islam totally forbids alcohol. It is haram to drink alcohol, and also to have anything to do with it, e.g. growing wine grapes, making alcohol or selling it.

Activity 1

List the points the quotations from Muslim scriptures make about intoxicants.

Activity 2

What benefit could there be in drinking and gambling? When the Qur'an says 'their harm is far greater than their benefit', what could it be referring to? Do you agree?

What does Islam say about medical drugs?

Muslims are permitted to take medical drugs to heal themselves. They are allowed to take medicines that contain alcohol if no alternative drug is available.

The problems of addiction

Drug addiction is a worldwide problem. Pakistan, which is a Muslim country, has seen a horrific rise in heroin addiction. In 1981, 25 cases were recorded; in 1986 it rose to 500,000 and, recently, has been estimated at 1.5 million. With a population of 95 million, that is a frighteningly large amount. Although Shari'ah Law has harsh penalties for the misuse of alcohol and drugs, Muslim agencies work to try to educate people about the problem. They also employ social workers and doctors to treat addicts in rehabilitation centres.

MUSLIMS ALLOWED TO REFUSE TO SELL ALCOHOL

30 September 2007

Sainsbury's have agreed that Muslim employees in their supermarkets can refuse to handle alcohol on religious grounds. The case arose when Mustapha, a Muslim checkout worker, told a customer at the checkout that he could not serve him with alcohol because it was against his religion and they were in the holy month of Ramadan.

A spokesperson for Sainsbury's said, 'We try to do our best in terms of complying with the requirements of religions.'

The solution

Sainsbury's have said a Muslim can refuse to serve a person with alcohol at the checkout. All they need to do is to raise their hand, in the same way an under-18 checkout operator does for the supervisor's permission to sell drink. In the case of a Muslim, another checkout worker will step in and pass the bottle in front of the scanner.

Sainsbury's have also agreed that

Muslims do not have to stack shelves in the wine and spirits section if they do not wish to. Other duties can be given to them.

Objections?

This has solved a problem for Muslim employees but some senior Muslims were not happy. The Secretary of the British Muslim Council said, 'People who sell alcoholic beverages cannot be regarded as having sinned. They are just carrying out the requirement of the job in order to earn a living. Muslim employees have a duty to their employer and in supermarkets most people would accept that in selling alcohol you are merely passing it through a checkout. That is hardly going to count against you on the Day of Judgement.'

The director of the Muslim Institute said Sainsbury's was being very good about it but 'the fault lies with the employee who is exploiting and misusing their goodwill'.

Check you have learnt:

- what the Qur'an teaches about alcohol and drugs
- an example of how a Muslim's attitude to drugs and alcohol has affected their day-to-day life.

Activity 3

Debate the two sides of the Sainsbury's and Mustapha case. How would you have handled it if you were the store manager? Why?

TRY YOUR SKILL AT THIS

The (c) question:

Explain why drinking alcohol is discouraged in **one** *religion other than Christianity*. (8)

SKILLS COACHING 12

END OF CHAPTER 4 CHECK

✓ Check the (a) question

In this chapter about *Crime and punishment* you learnt these KEYWORDS:

addiction	capital punishment	crime	deterrence	judgement	justice
law	reform	rehabilitation	responsibility	retribution	sin

a) Write three sentences, each using one of the keywords from the list above, to show you understand the meaning of three keywords.

b) Work with a partner to test each other on the meaning of the keywords in this chapter.

✓ Check the (c) question

We have looked at the attitudes of government, society and Christians and Muslims towards:

- law and justice
- capital punishment
- drugs and alcohol

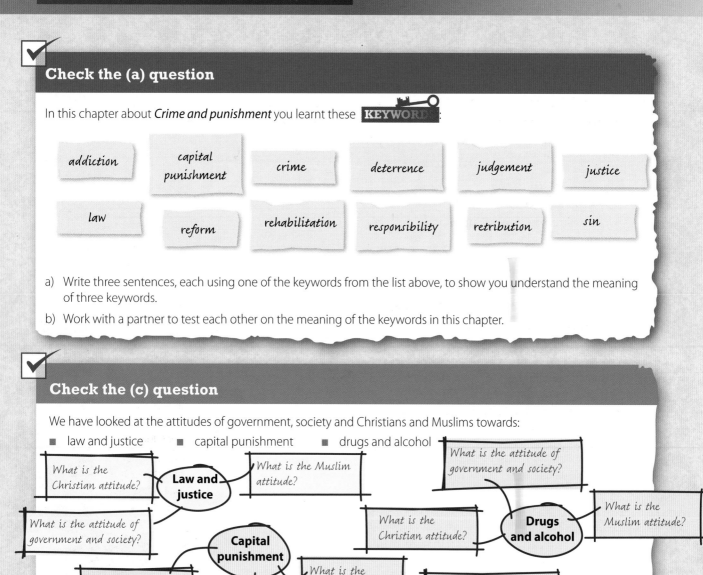

Law and justice
- What is the Christian attitude?
- What is the Muslim attitude?
- What is the attitude of government and society?

Capital punishment
- What is the Christian attitude?
- What is the Muslim attitude?
- What is the attitude of government and society?

Drugs and alcohol
- What is the attitude of government and society?
- What is the Muslim attitude?
- What is the Christian attitude?

Copy and complete the three spider diagrams to check your understanding.

✓ Check the (b) and (d) questions

Check you know different people's responses to the issues above for the (b) and (d) questions.

Remind yourself of the two or three reasons the other side gives to argue against you.

Obviously, your responses to the issues above are the most important ones. Rehearse two or three reasons you would give to support your viewpoint on each issue.

Finally, the vitally important thing, what religious viewpoint are you going to use for each issue?

Here is a typical example of how questions about *Crime and punishment* might be presented on the exam paper. Choose one of these questions to work through in exam conditions in order to check your progress.

Before the exam, remember to:

☑ learn the correct definitions for all keywords

☑ revise thoroughly all you need to know. You can use Skills coaching sections 3, 6, 9 and 12 to help you

☑ keep practising the understanding and evaluative skills you have learnt.

SECTION 4 – CRIME AND PUNISHMENT
You must answer ONE question from this section.

EITHER

7 (a) What is meant by **rehabilitation**? (2)

(b) 'Criminals should be made to apologize to their victims.'
Do you agree? Give **two** reasons for your point of view. (4)

(c) Explain the problems caused to society and to a person's health by the misuse of alcohol. (8)

(d) 'Capital punishment can never be justified.'
In your answer you should refer to at least one religion.
(i) Do you agree? Give reasons for your opinion. (3)
(ii) Give reasons why some people may disagree with you. (3)
(Total for Question 7 = 20 marks)

OR

8 (a) What is meant by **sin**? (2)

(b) 'God will judge a person's behaviour, nobody else should.'
Do you agree? Give **two** reasons for your point of view. (4)

(c) Explain the different attitudes Christians have to capital punishment. (8)

(d) 'People should be free to drink if they want to.'
In your answer you should refer to at least one religion.
(i) Do you agree? Give reasons for your opinion. (3)
(ii) Give reasons why some people may disagree with you. (3)
(Total for Question 8 = 20 marks)

During the exam, remember to:

☑ plan your answers step by step

☑ use full sentences and good English

☑ spend 20 minutes on each question

☑ use the final 10 minutes of the exam to check everything through.

If this had been the real exam, how well would you have done? Use the marking grid to check your progress. Answers to (a) appear on page 99, the grid for (b) is on page 31, the grid for (c) is on page 30 and the grid for (d) is on page 31.

Keyword glossary

addiction a recurring compulsion to engage in an activity regardless of its bad effects

aggression attacking without being provoked

artificial insemination injecting semen into the uterus by artificial means

Bible the holy book of Christians

bullying intimidating/frightening people weaker than yourself

capital punishment the death penalty for a crime or offence

Church the community of Christians (with a small c it means a Christian place of worship)

conflict resolution bringing a fight or struggle to a peaceful conclusion

conscience an inner feeling of the rightness or wrongness of an action

conservation protecting and preserving natural resources and the environment

creation the act of creating the universe or the universe which has been created

crime an act against the law

the Decalogue the Ten Commandments

democratic processes the ways in which all citizens can take part in government (usually through elections)

deterrence the idea that punishments should be of such a nature that they will put people off (deter) committing crimes

electoral processes the ways in which voting is organized

embryo a fertilized egg in the first eight weeks after conception

environment the surroundings in which plants and animals live and on which they depend to live

exploitation taking advantage of a weaker group

forgiveness stopping blaming someone and/or pardoning them for what they have done wrong

global warming the increase in the temperature of the earth's atmosphere (thought to be caused by the greenhouse effect)

the Golden Rule the teaching of Jesus that you should treat others as you would like them to treat you

human rights the rights and freedoms to which everyone is entitled

infertility not being able to have children

in-vitro fertilization the method of fertilizing a human egg in a test tube

judgement the act of judging people and their actions

just war a war which is fought for the right reasons and in a right way

justice due allocation of reward and punishment/the maintenance of what is right

law rules made by Parliament and enforceable by the courts

natural resources naturally occurring materials, such as oil and fertile land, which can be used by humans

organ donation giving organs to be used in transplant surgery

pacifism the belief that all disputes should be settled by peaceful means

political party a group which tries to be elected into power on the basis of its policies (e.g. Labour, Conservative)

pressure group a group formed to influence government policy on a particular issue

reconciliation bringing together people who were opposed to each other

reform the idea that punishments should try to change criminals so that they will not commit crimes again

rehabilitation restore to normal life

respect treating a person or their feelings with consideration

responsibility being responsible for one's actions

retribution the idea that punishments should make criminals pay for what they have done wrong

sin an act against the will of God

Situation Ethics the idea that Christians should base moral decisions on what is the most loving thing to do

social change the way in which society has changed and is changing (and also the possibilities for future change)

stewardship looking after something so it can be passed on to the next generation

surrogacy an arrangement whereby a woman bears a child on behalf of another woman

the United Nations an international body set up to promote world peace and cooperation

weapons of mass destruction weapons which can destroy large areas and numbers of people

world peace the ending of war throughout the whole world (the basic aim of the United Nations)